ESL Grades 4–6

D1524557

Contents

Introduction

The *ESL Standards for Pre-K–12 Students* notes that "what is most important for ESOL learners is to function effectively in English and through English while learning challenging academic content." (p. 6) The Steck-Vaughn *ESL* series was designed to meet the needs of both second-language learners and teachers in achieving this goal.

To help ESOL students, the lessons in *ESL*:
• introduce concepts in context.
• highlight specific words or concepts with bold print and rebus clues.
• reinforce the skill with practice.

To help the teacher, the lessons in *ESL*:
• target grade-appropriate concepts.
• offer step-by-step instruction on beginning, intermediate, and advanced levels.
• build background knowledge.
• suggest ideas or words to be shared in the student's native language.
• signal when a phonics skill is unfamiliar to speakers of a specific language.
• point out idioms and multiple-meaning words that could cause confusion.
• suggest extension activities that apply the skill in a real-world situation.

THE ESOL STUDENT

Like all students, second-language learners bring to the classroom a wide variety of experiences, history, and culture. It is important to help these students feel appreciated and respected in the classroom. They have a wealth of knowledge that is interesting and beneficial to all students. By asking them to share stories and experiences about their native country as well as expressions and words in their native language, you will help them feel productive and successful.

 The multicultural icon in the lessons indicates ways for students to share aspects of their language and culture with the class.

ESOL students have different proficiency levels of the English language. Three levels are generally recognized.

Beginning: Students at this level have little or no understanding of the English language. They respond to questions and commands nonverbally by pointing or drawing. Some students at this level may give single word responses. They depend on nonprint clues to decode information in texts. To facilitate learning for beginning language learners, ask questions to which students can gesture to answer or respond with a "yes" or "no." Instruction should be slow, directed, and repetitive.

Intermediate: Intermediate ESOL students have a fundamental grasp of English. They understand and can use basic vocabulary associated with routine situations and needs. These students can respond using simple sentences, but their grammar is inconsistent. To read text, these language learners must have prior knowledge of the concepts. To facilitate learning for intermediate language learners, ask questions to which students can reply with words or short phrases. Instruction should be directed at first to make sure students understand the directions, and the page should be read to insure they know the content. It is also helpful to pair students.

Advanced: Students at this level are able to understand and communicate using English in most routine situations. They may need explanations of idioms, multiple-meaning words, and abstract concepts. They are often fluent readers and writers of English. Instruction for these learners includes responding to higher-level questions and reading the directions and explaining words and phrases that might be confusing.

ORGANIZATION OF *ESL*

The *ESL* book is divided into four units.

Readiness: This section reinforces the basic skills students will need in the classroom and many real-world situations. There are two parts to each lesson. Part A introduces the skill or concept with picture clues and bold print to help second-language learners focus on the important words. Part B offers practice in a real-life application.

Phonics: This unit introduces grade-appropriate phonics skills. Each lesson has three sections. Part A introduces the skill or concept with picture clues and bold print words. Part B reinforces the words and the sounds from part A. In part C, students apply the skill. The phonics lessons also identify sounds that some language learners may be unfamiliar with.

 The whirling letter icon indicates multiple-meaning words that may confuse students.

Language Arts: Like the phonics unit, this unit focuses on skills that are grade-appropriate. It also offers instruction in three parts: introduction, reinforcement, and application.

Vocabulary: The vocabulary unit highlights basic words and background knowledge students need to function on a daily level or to understand topics taught in other curriculum areas. Like the readiness unit, two-part lessons first introduce the concept and then give practice applying it.

SPECIAL FEATURES

Individual Student Chart: The Individual Student Chart found on page 3 can help you track each student's skill understanding and progress.

Lessons: Each lesson in Units 2, 3, and 4 is a two-page spread. The left page is the model for teaching the pupil activity sheet, found on the right page. The teacher model explains how to focus on the skill or ways to build background knowledge. Most importantly, the teacher model suggests the steps for teaching the page at each proficiency level.

Certificates: The two certificates on page 122 can be copied and distributed to students. One recognizes the student's efforts, and the other commends the student for successfully attaining a skill.

Take-Home Book: Beginning on page 123, you will find a take-home book about important American symbols. Copies can be distributed to students. You may wish to read aloud the booklet several times before sending it home with students.

Individual Student Chart

Name _____

Skill	Accomplished (yes/no)	Date Page Completed
Unit 1: Readiness		
In, On, Beside, and Under		
Top, Middle, and Bottom		
Left and Right		
Same and Different		
First, Next, and Last		
Numbers to 10		
Number Words		
Numbers to 20		
Counting by Tens		
Large Numbers		
Capital Letters		
Lowercase Letters		
Partner Letters		
Letters and Sounds		
More Letters and Sounds		
A Name		
An Address		
A Telephone Number		
An Internet Address		
Directions		
More Directions		
Unit 2: Phonics		
Short a		
Short e		
Short i		
Short o		
Short u		
Long a (a_e)		
Long a (ay and ai)		
Long e (ee and ea)		
Long i (i_e and ie)		
Long o (o_e)		
Long o (oa and oe)		
Long u (u_e)		
y as a Vowel		
r-Controlled Vowel ar		

Skill	Accomplished (yes/no)	Date Page Completed
r-Controlled Vowel or		
r-Controlled Vowels er, ir, ur		
Vowel Digraph ea		
Vowel Digraphs au, aw, al, all		
Diphthong ow		
Sounds of c		
Sounds of g		
Sounds of s		
Digraphs ch and wh		
Digraphs sh and th		
Unit 3: Language Arts		
Nouns		
Proper Nouns		
Plurals		
Present Tense Verbs		
Past Tense Verbs		
Pronouns		
Adjectives That Compare		
Compound Words		
Contractions		
Prefixes		
Suffixes		
Unit 4: Vocabulary		
Community		
Days of the Week		
Family Words		
Furniture		
Land and Water		
Machines		
Money		
School Rooms		
Senses		
Shapes		
Sports		
Time		
Weather		

Sample Readiness Lesson

The following lesson can be used as a model for teaching the activity pages in the Readiness unit.

PREPARATION

Preview Part A on the activity page. Duplicate the picture/item shown, either by drawing the item on the board, displaying a magazine picture, or better yet, showing the actual item. Students will need to become familiar with these items before learning concepts. Moreover, it is very important that they actively participate in the learning by moving something or by pantomiming. It will help them better understand the vocabulary and concept.

INTRODUCTION

Display the item and say a short, simple sentence about the concept as it relates to the item. Have students repeat the sentence. Introduce all the vocabulary and encourage students to actively participate as they repeat the words. Write the words on the board.

Beginning

Part A: Distribute the page. Direct students to look at the picture. Read the words or sentence aloud and have students repeat the words as they point to the picture. Ask questions about the picture to which students can respond with a nonverbal response or a yes/no answer.

Part B: Explain what students will do in Part B. Have them point to the first picture or word. Identify the picture name or word for students to repeat. Direct students through each step to find and write the answer. Again, if possible, have students actively participate in the process. Repeat with each picture or word.

Intermediate

Part A: Distribute the page. Direct students to look at the picture. Read the words or sentence aloud and have students repeat. Ask questions about the picture to which students can choose one of two answers or the answer can be found in a visual clue.

Part B: Explain what students will do in Part B. Have them point to the first picture or word. Identify the picture name or word for students to repeat. Ask questions that help students find and write the answer. After modeling how to do the work, read each remaining problem, but pause for students to find and write the answer on their own.

Advanced

Part A: Distribute the page. Direct students to look at the picture. Read the sentence aloud and have students repeat it. Invite students to talk about the picture. Encourage vocabulary development and practice as students talk.

Part B: Read aloud the directions. Ask students to skim the page to see if they have a question about any of the words or pictures. Have students complete the page independently.

In, On, Beside, and Under

A. Study the pictures and words.

| in | on | beside | under |

B. Write words from the box to complete the sentences.

| in | on | beside | under |

1. This cat is _____ the desk.

2. This cat is _____ the desk.

3. This cat is _____ the desk.

4. This cat is _____ the desk.

Top, Middle, and Bottom

A. Study the picture and words.

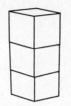

top
middle
bottom

B. Write words from the box to complete the sentences.

top	middle	bottom

1. The boxes are on the _____ shelf.

2. The bags are on the _____ shelf.

3. The cans are on the _____ shelf.

4. The oranges are in the _____ box.

5. The apples are in the _____ box.

6. The bananas are in the _____ box.

Left and Right

A. Study the picture and words.

left   **right**

B. Tell the way the truck will turn to get to the post office. Write **left** or **right** in the boxes.

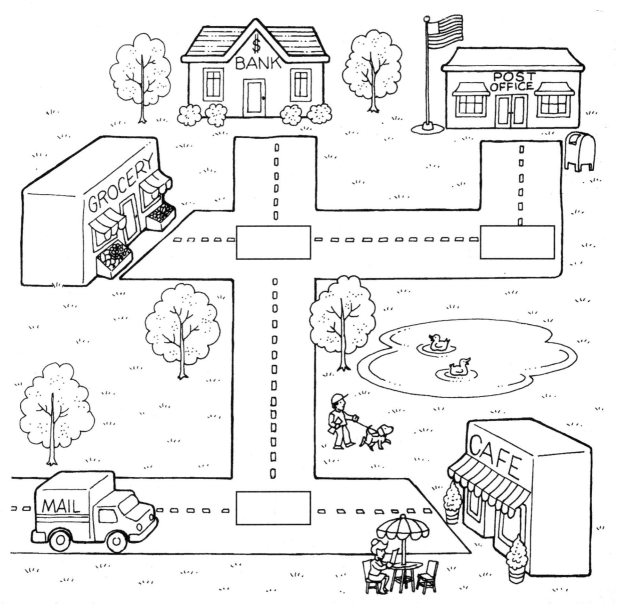

Same and Different

A. Read the sentences.

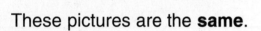

These pictures are the **same**.   These pictures are **different**.

B. Tell if the computer pictures are the same or different. Write **same** or **different**.

1.

_____

2.

_____

3.

_____

4.

_____

5.

_____

6.

_____

First, Next, and Last

A. Study the pictures and words.

first

next

last

B. Draw animals in each place. Write **first**, **next**, and **last** to tell the order that you would visit the animals.

Numbers to 10

A. Study the pictures and numbers.

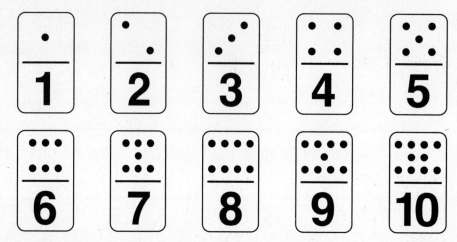

B. Choose eight dominoes from above. Draw the dots and write the numerals. Then, play dominoes with a partner. Say the numbers as you play.

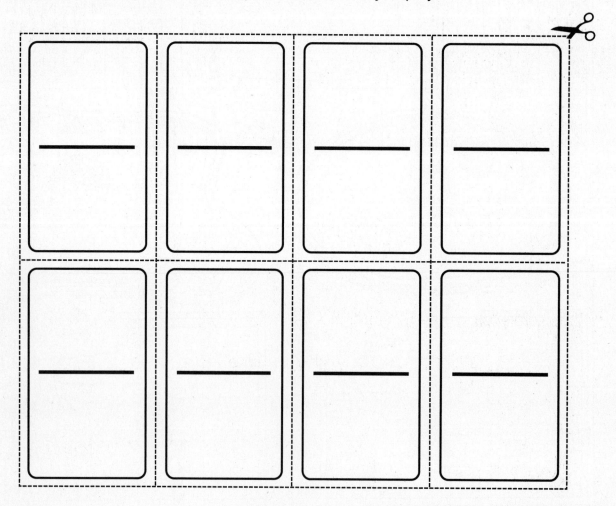

Name _____   Date _____

Number Words

A. Study the numbers and words.

1	2	3	4	5	6	7	8	9	10
one	two	three	four	five	six	seven	eight	nine	ten

B. Write the word name for each number.

Name _____ Date _____

Numbers to 20

A. 1 2 3 4 5 6 7 8 9 10
        11 12 13 14 15 16 17 18 19 20

B. Draw lines to the numbers in order.

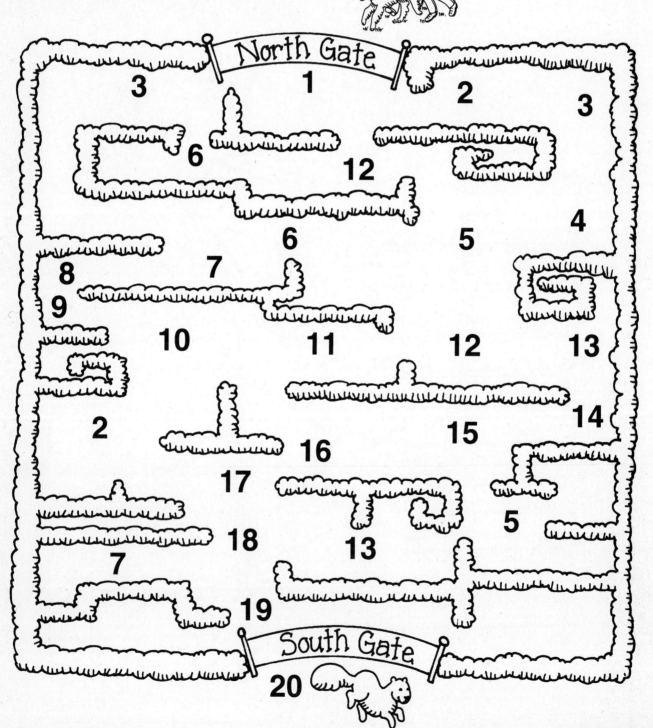

Counting by Tens

A. Study the picture and words.

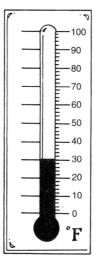

one hundred
ninety
eighty
seventy
sixty
fifty
forty
thirty
twenty
ten
zero

It is **30**°F outside.

B. Write the number and number word for the temperature shown.

1.
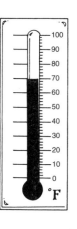

_____

2.

_____

3.
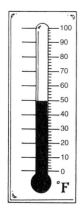

_____

4.
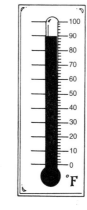

_____

Large Numbers

A. Study the pictures and words.

100
one hundred

1,000
one thousand

B. Write the number and the number word to tell how many.

1.

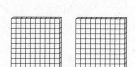

<u>   200   </u>
<u>two hundred</u>

2.

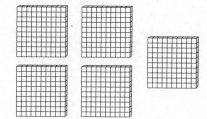

_____

_____

3.

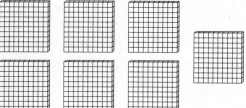

_____

_____

4.

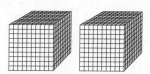

_____

_____

5.

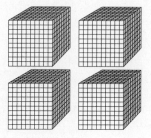

_____

_____

6.

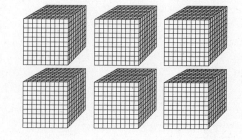

_____

_____

Capital Letters

A. Study the letters.

A B C D E F G H I J K L M N O P Q R S T U V W X Y Z

ABCDEFGHIJKLMNOPQRSTUVWXYZ

B. Connect the dots in **ABC** order. Then, write the capital letters in cursive.

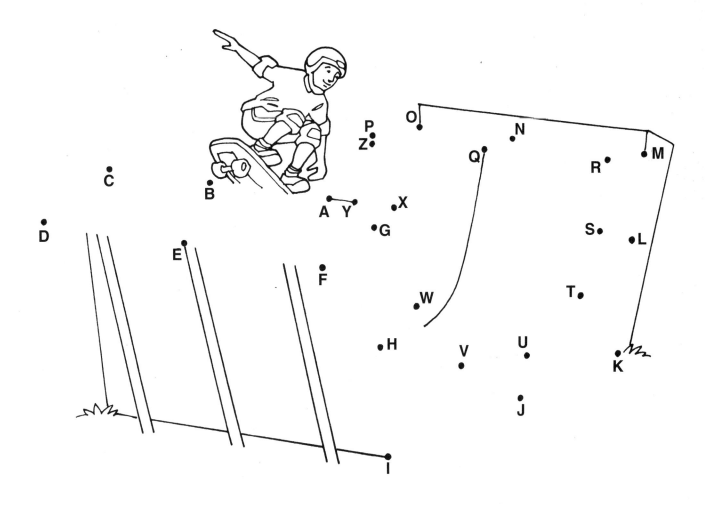

a _____

_____

Lowercase Letters

A. Study the letters.

a b c d e f g h i j k l m n o p q r s t u v w x y z

a b c d e f g h i j k l m n o p q r s t u v w x y z

B. Connect the dots in **abc** order. Then, write the lowercase letters in cursive.

a _____

_____

Name _____ Date _____

Partner Letters

A. Study the letters.

Aa	Bb	Cc	Dd		Ee	Ff	Gg	Hh	Ii	Jj	Kk	Ll	Mm
Nn	Oo	Pp	Qq		Rr	Ss	Tt	Uu	Vv	Ww	Xx	Yy	Zz

B. The frog eats only the flies that have partner letters on their bodies. Color those flies. Then count how many flies the frog eats.

How many flies does the frog eat? _____

Name _____   Date _____

Letters and Sounds

A. Read the sentence.

It is time for **lunch**.

B. Circle the letter that stands for the beginning sound in the picture name.

1.   t   m   d

2.   c   z   h

3.   g   r   s

4.   n   z   q

5.   r   w   j

6.   b   f   k

7.   v   x   h

8.   y   g   v

9.   w   l   p

More Letters and Sounds

A. Read the sentence.

A **<u>bike</u>** moves fast.

B. Circle the letter that stands for the beginning sound in the picture name.

1.

t   m   d

2.

SCHOOL BUS

b   w   h

3.

g   r   s

4.

p   z   q

5.

r   w   j

6.

g   f   c

7.

v   x   h

8.

y   s   v

9.

w   l   p

Name _____   Date _____

A Name

A. Read the sentences.

My **name** is Marco Fuentes.
The **name** of my friend is Rob Wilson.

B. Write your name on the T-shirt. Then, color the shirt. Work with friends to complete the sentences.

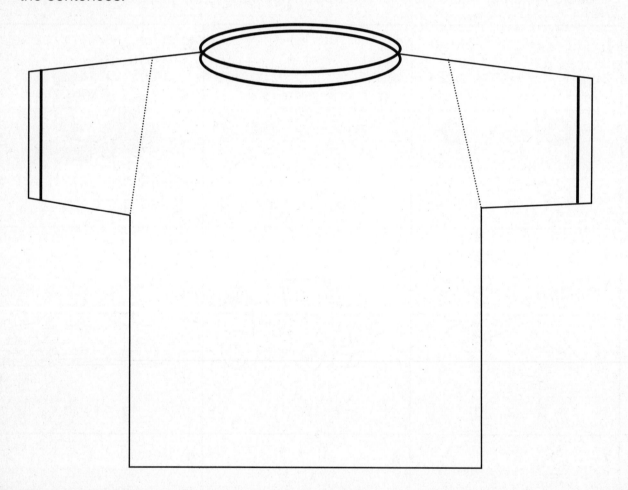

My name is _____.

The name of my friend is _____.

The name of my friend is _____.

The name of my friend is _____.

www.svschoolsupply.com
© Steck-Vaughn Company

Name _____   Date _____

An Address

A.

Marco Fuentes
123 South Street
Raleigh, North Carolina 27613

Rob Wilson
1243 Maple Street
Portland, Oregon 97219

My **address** is 123 South Street.

B. Write your address on the mailbox. Work with a partner to complete the envelope.

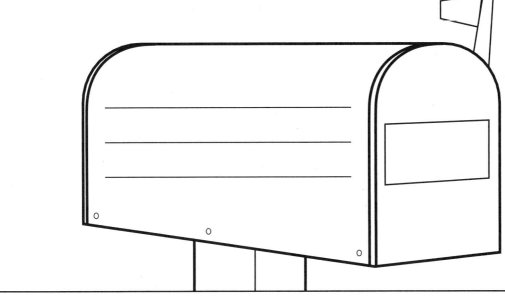

Name _____   Date _____

A Telephone Number

A.

My **telephone number** is 555-2648.
The **telephone number** for Rob is 555-9753.

B. Color the buttons that show your telephone number.
Work with friends to complete the sentences.

My telephone number is _____.

The telephone number for _____ is

_____.

The telephone number for _____ is

_____.

The telephone number for _____ is

_____.

An Internet Address

A. Read the sentence.

⬅	➡	⬇	✖	http://www.ask.com
BACK	**FORWARD**	**REFRESH**	**STOP**	

The **Internet address** is www.ask.com.

B. What animal do you want to know more about? Draw a picture of it. Write a question about it. Then, go to the Internet site above on a computer. Ask your question. Visit other sites. Write the addresses of the places you visit.

Question: _____

_____

I visited the Internet site _____.

I visited the Internet site _____.

I visited the Internet site _____.

Directions

A.

look   **listen**   **raise hand**   **say**

B. Look at each picture. Write a word from above to tell what is happening in the picture.

1.

_____

2.

_____

3.

_____

4.

_____

Name _____   Date _____

More Directions

A.

(**circle**)   **underline**   write ✏   color 🖍

B. Circle the ⚾. Underline the 🖍. Write your name on the 🏠.

Color the 🍎.

Short *a*

NOTE: Students whose native language is Italian may have problems with the short *a* sound.

INTRODUCTION

Display a baseball bat. Say: *This is a bat.* Have students repeat the sentence. Then, ask students what you have. Pass the bat to each student and say, *(Name) has a bat.* Encourage students to repeat the sentence each time. Say *bat* again, stressing the middle sound: */b/-/a/-/a/-/t/.* Explain that /a/ is the short *a* sound.

 Invite students to share the word *bat* in their native language.

 The homograph *bat* may confuse students. If possible, provide a picture of a flying bat. Explain that *bat* has two meanings. Say simple sentences that provide context clues of the word's use. (*The bat has wings. Mei has a ball and a bat.*) Have students point to the picture of the flying bat or the wooden bat to show an understanding of the way the word is used.

Beginning

Part A: Distribute page 27. Direct students to look at the first picture. Read the sentence aloud and have students repeat it. Pass the bat to each student and have the student repeat the sentence. Then, ask the following questions about the picture:
• *Does Pat have a bat? Point to it.*
• *Does Pat have a cap? Point to it.*

Repeat the sentence, stressing the short *a* sound in each word: */p/-/a/-/a/-/t/ /h/-/a/-/a/-/z/ a /c/-/a/-/a/-/p/ /a/-/a/-/nd/ a /b/-/a/-/a/-/t/.* Tell students that *Pat, has, cap, and,* and *bat* all have the short *a* sound. Point out that the words *cap* and *bat* are in dark print.

Part B: Tell students they will write words that name pictures. Have students point to the bat and say the picture name. Then, have students point to the words in dark print in the sentence above. Ask questions that help students choose and write the word *bat.* Repeat with the picture of the cap.

Part C: Tell students they will choose words whose names have the short *a* sound to complete sentences. Read aloud the first sentence with the rebus. Say *pan* again, stressing the short *a* sound: */p/-/a/-/a/-/n/.* Explain to students that *pan* has the short *a* sound. Then, say *pan* again for them to repeat. Tell students that *pan* is spelled *p, a, n.* Help them find the word in the list, write it on the line, and cross out the word once it is chosen. Continue the process with the remaining sentences.

Intermediate

Part A: Follow the directions in Part A of the Beginning section, but substitute these questions:
• *Does Pat have a fan or a bat?*
• *Does Pat have a cap or a lamp?*

Part B: Tell students they will write words that name pictures. Then, help students identify the pictures. Have them complete the section with a partner.

Part C: Tell students they will choose words whose names have the short *a* sound to complete sentences. Say the word *map*, stressing the short *a* sound: */m/-/a/-/a/-/p/.* Say the word again and have students repeat the word as they point to it. Then, repeat the process with the other words. Explain that all the words in the box have the short *a* sound. Next, read aloud the first sentence with the rebus. Pause to allow students time to write their answer. Continue the process with the remaining sentences.

Advanced

Part A: Distribute page 27. Direct students to look at the first picture. Read the sentence aloud and have students repeat it. Invite students to talk about the picture. Repeat the sentence, stressing the short *a* sound in each word: */p/-/a/-/a/-/t/ /h/-/a/-/a/-/z/ a /c/-/a/-/a/-/p/ /a/-/a/-/nd/ a /b/-/a/-/a/-/t/.* Tell students that *Pat, has, cap, and,* and *bat* all have the short *a* sound. Point out that the words *cap* and *bat* are in dark print.

Parts B and C: Read aloud the directions. Ask students to skim the page to see if they have a question about any of the words. Have students complete the page independently.

EXTENSION

Have students draw a picture of something that has the short *a* sound. Then, invite them to play a cumulative memory game. Have students pass a grocery bag, name their drawing, put it in the bag, and repeat a list of the other pictures already in the bag. Play continues until each student has had a turn.

Name _____ Date _____

Short *a*

A. Read the sentence.

Pat has a **cap** and a **bat**.

B. Write the name of each picture. Use the words in dark print above.

1.

_____

2.

_____

C. Write a word from the box to complete each sentence.

| map   pan   gas |

3. Pat has a 🍳 _____.

4. Pat looks at a 🗺 _____.

5. Pat gets ⛽ _____.

Short *e*

NOTE: Students whose native language is Urdu may have problems with the short *e* sound.

INTRODUCTION

Display a picture of a hen. Say: *This is a hen*. Have students repeat the sentence. Then, ask students what sound a hen makes. Tell students that you will say a list of words. Ask them to make the sound of a hen when they hear the word *hen*. Then, slowly say: *cow, hen, cat, hen, goat, dog, hen*. Display the picture again and say *hen*, stressing the middle sound: */h/-/e/-/e/-/n/*. Explain that */e/* is the short *e* sound.

 The sound a hen makes may be different in other languages. Point out the sounds as students name them. Read the word list above several times, choosing a different hen sound for students to make.

Beginning

Part A: Distribute page 29. Direct students to look at the first picture. Read the sentence aloud and have students repeat it. Pass the picture of the hen to each student and have the student repeat the sentence. Then, ask the following questions about the picture:
• *Where is the hen? Point to it.*
• *What is on the nest? Point to it.*
• *Is the hen in a bed?*
• *Is the hen on a nest?*

Repeat the sentence, stressing the short *e* sound in each word: *The /h/-/e/-/e/-/n/ sat on a /n/-/e/-/e/-/st/*. Tell students that *hen* and *nest* have the short *e* sound. Point out that the words *hen* and *nest* are in dark print.

Part B: Tell students they will write words that name pictures. Have students point to the nest and say the picture name. Then, have students point to the words in dark print in the sentence above. Ask questions that help students choose and write the word *nest*. Repeat with the picture of the hen.

Part C: Tell students they will choose words whose names have the short *e* sound to complete sentences. Read aloud the first sentence with the

rebus. Say *desk* again, stressing the short *e* sound: */d/-/e/-/e/-/sk/*. Explain to students that *desk* has the short *e* sound. Then, say *desk* again for them to repeat. Tell students that *desk* is spelled *d, e, s, k*. Help them find the word in the list, write it on the line, and cross out the word once it is chosen. Continue the process with the remaining sentences.

Intermediate

Part A: Follow the directions in Part A of the Beginning section, but substitute these questions:
• *What is on the nest?*
• *Where is the hen?*

Part B: Tell students they will write words that name pictures. Then, help students identify the pictures. Have them complete the section with a partner.

Part C: Tell students they will choose words whose names have the short *e* sound to complete sentences. Say the word *vet*, stressing the short *e* sound: */v/-/e/-/e/-/t/*. Say the word again and have students repeat the word as they point to it. Then, repeat the process with the other words. Explain that all the words in the box have the short *e* sound. Next, read aloud the first sentence with the rebus. Pause to allow students time to write their answer. Continue the process with the remaining sentences.

Advanced

Part A: Distribute page 29. Direct students to look at the first picture. Read the sentence aloud and have students repeat it. Invite students to talk about the picture. Repeat the sentence, stressing the short *e* sound in each word: The */h/-/e/-/e/-/n/ sat on a /n/-/e/-/e/-/st/*. Tell students that *hen* and *nest* have the short *e* sound. Point out that the words *hen* and *nest* are in dark print.

Parts B and C: Read aloud the directions. Ask the students to skim the page to see if they have a question about any of the words. Have students complete the page independently.

EXTENSION

Have students draw a picture of a hen sitting on something else in which the name has the short *e* sound.

Short *e*

A. Read the sentence.

The **hen** sat on a **nest**.

B. Write the name of each picture. Use the words in dark print above.

1.

_____

2.

_____

C. Write a word from the box to complete each sentence.

vet   egg   desk

3. The hen sat on a _____.

4. The hen has an _____.

5. The hen went to a _____.

Short *i*

NOTE: Students whose native language is Greek, Italian, or Japanese may have problems with the short *i* sound.

INTRODUCTION

Draw an outline of a pig on the board. Say: *This is a pig.* Have students repeat the sentence. Then, tell students that you are going to tell a story about three pigs. Ask them to raise their hand each time they hear the word *pig*. Then, slowly tell the story of *The Three Little Pigs*, acting out some of the actions of the more difficult words. After the story, say *pig* again, stressing the middle sound: */p/-/i/-/i/-/g/*. Explain that /i/ is the short *i* sound.

 Invite students to share the word *pig* in their native language.

 Some students may hear /o/ or /u/ in words having the short *i* sound.

Beginning

Part A: Distribute page 31. Direct students to look at the first picture. Read the sentence aloud and have students repeat it. Invite each student to repeat the sentence. Then, ask the following questions about the picture:
• *What is digging? Point to it.*
• *What can the pig do? Show me.*

Repeat the sentence, stressing the short *i* sound in each word: *The /p/-/i/-/i/-/g/ can /d/-/i/-/i/-/g/.* Tell students that *pig* and *dig* have the short *i* sound. Point out that the words *pig* and *dig* are in dark print.

Part B: Tell students they will write words that name pictures. Have students point to the pig and say the picture name. Then, have students point to the words in dark print in the sentence above. Ask questions that help students choose and write the word *pig*. Repeat with the picture of dig.

Part C: Tell students they will change a letter in words so that the new words have the short *i* sound. Identify the picture of the pin. Have students repeat the word. Say the picture name

again, stressing the short *i* sound: */p/-/i/-/i/-/n/*. Then, have students point to the word under the picture. Ask questions that help students understand that they must change the *a* to an *i* to make the word *pin*. Next, spell *pin* out loud. Continue the process with the remaining pictures.

Intermediate

Part A: Follow the directions in Part A of the Beginning section, but substitute these questions:
• *What can dig?*
• *What can the pig do?*

Part B: Tell students they will write words that name pictures. Then, help students identify the pictures. Have them complete the section with a partner.

Part C: Tell students they will change a letter in words so that the new words have the short *i* sound. Identify the picture of the pin. Have students repeat the word. Say the picture name again, stressing the short *i* sound: */p/-/i/-/i/-/n/*. Then, have students point to the word under the picture. Say the word. Pause to let students write the new word. Next, spell *pin* out loud. Continue the process with the remaining pictures.

Advanced

Part A: Distribute page 31. Direct students to look at the first picture. Read the sentence aloud and have students repeat it. Invite students to talk about the picture. Repeat the sentence, stressing the short *i* sound in each word: *The /p/-/i/-/i/-/g/ can /d/-/i/-/i/-/g/.* Tell students that *pig* and *dig* have the short *i* sound. Point out that the words *pig* and *dig* are in dark print.

Parts B and C: Read aloud the directions. Ask students to skim the page to see if they have a question about any of the words. Have students complete the page independently.

EXTENSION

Invite students to act out the story of *The Three Little Pigs* as you retell it.

Name _____ Date _____

Short *i*

A. Read the sentence.

 The **pig** can **dig**.

B. Write the name of each picture. Use the words in dark print above.

1.

_____

2.

_____

C. Change one letter in each word so that it names the picture. Write the new word.

3.

pan _____

4.

hat _____

5.

clap _____

6.

wag _____

Short o

INTRODUCTION

Display a block in a pot. Say: *The block is in the pot.* Have students repeat the sentence. Then, put the pot on the floor and invite students to stand back from the pot and take turns tossing the block into it. Encourage students to repeat the sentence when they get the block in the pot. Say *pot* again, stressing the middle sound: */p/-/o/-/o/-/t/*. Explain that /o/ is the short *o* sound.

 Invite students to share the word *pot* in their native language and to describe a food they like to cook in a pot.

 Some students may hear /ō/ or /aw/ in words having the short *o* sound.

Beginning

Part A: Distribute page 33. Direct students to look at the first picture. Read the sentence aloud and have students repeat it. Pantomime touching the pot as if it is hot and repeat the sentence. Then, ask the following questions about the picture:
• *What is hot? Point to it.*
• *How does the pot feel if you touch it? Show me.*

Repeat the sentence, stressing the short *o* sound in each word: *The /p/-/o/-/o/-/t/ is /h/-/o/-/o/-/t/.* Tell students that *pot* and *hot* both have the short *o* sound. Point out that the words *pot* and *hot* are in dark print.

Part B: Tell students they will write words that name pictures. Have students point to the hot pot and say *hot*. Then, have students point to the words in dark print in the sentence above. Ask questions that help students choose and write the word *hot*. Repeat with the picture of the pot.

Part C: Tell students they will change a letter in words so that the new words have the short *o* sound. Identify the picture of the fox. Have students repeat the word. Say the picture name again, stressing the short *o* sound: */f/-/o/-/o/-/x/*. Then, have students point to the word under the picture. Say the word. Ask questions that help

students understand that they must change the *i* to an *o* to make the word *fox*. Next, spell *fox* out loud. Continue the process with the remaining pictures.

Intermediate

Part A: Follow the directions in Part A of the Beginning section, but substitute these questions:
• *Is the pot hot or cold?*
• *Is a mop or pot hot?*

Part B: Tell students they will write words that name pictures. Then, help students identify the pictures. Have them complete the section with a partner.

Part C: Tell students they will change a letter in words so that the new words have the short *o* sound. Identify the picture of the fox. Have students repeat the word. Say the picture name again, stressing the short *o* sound: */f/-/o/-/o/-/x/*. Then, have students point to the word under the picture. Say the word. Pause to let students write the new word. Next, spell *fox* out loud. Continue the process with the remaining pictures.

Advanced

Part A: Distribute page 33. Direct students to look at the first picture. Read the sentence aloud and have students repeat it. Invite students to talk about the picture. Repeat the sentence, stressing the short *o* sound in each word: *The /p/-/o/-/o/-/t/ is /h/-/o/-/o/-/t/.* Tell students that *pot* and *hot* both have the short *o* sound. Point out that the words *pot* and *hot* are in dark print.

Parts B and C: Read aloud the directions. Ask students to skim the page to see if they have a question about any of the words. Have students complete the page independently.

EXTENSION

Challenge students to search for items that have the short *o* sound to place in the pot. As students return with an item, have them complete the following sentence frame as they put the item in the pot: *[Item] is in the pot.*

Name _____ Date _____

Short o

A. Read the sentence.

The **pot** is **hot**.

B. Write the name of each picture. Use the words in dark print above.

1.

_____

2.

_____

C. Change one letter in each word so that it names the picture. Write the new word.

3.

fix _____

4.

tip _____

5.

dig _____

6.

hip _____

Short *u*

INTRODUCTION

Take students outside. Ask: *How fast can you run?* Have each student repeat the sentence and then run to a designated spot and back. Once back to the classroom, say *run*, stressing the middle sound: /r/-/u/-/u/-/n/. Explain that /u/ is the short *u* sound.

 Invite students to say the word *run* in their native language.

 The homograph *duck* may confuse students. Explain that *duck* has two meanings. Say simple sentences that provide context clues of the word's use. (*The duck swims in the water. Duck if the ball comes your way.*) Have students quack like a duck or duck down behind their desk to show an understanding of the way the word is used.

Beginning

Part A: Distribute page 35. Direct students to look at the picture of the duck that is running. Read the sentence aloud and have students repeat it. Invite partners to pantomime running as they repeat the sentence. Then, ask the following questions about the picture:
• *What is running? Point to it.*
• *How does the duck move? Show me.*
• *Is the duck jumping?*
• *Is the duck running?*

Repeat the sentence, stressing the short *u* sound in each word: *The /d/-/u/-/u/-/k/ can /r/-/u/-/u/-/n/.* Tell students that *duck* and *run* have the short *u* sound. Point out that the words *duck* and *run* are in dark print.

Part B: Tell students they will write words that name pictures. Have students point to the boy who runs and say the picture name. Then, have students point to the words in dark print in the sentence above. Ask questions that help students choose and write the word *run*. Repeat with the picture of the duck.

Part C: Tell students they will choose words whose names have the short *u* sound to complete sentences. Read aloud the first sentence with the

rebus. Say *up* again, stressing the short *u* sound: /u/-/u/-/p/. Explain to students that *up* has the short *u* sound. Then, say *up* again for them to repeat. Tell students that *up* is spelled *u, p*. Help them find the word in the list, write it on the line, and cross out the word once it is chosen. Continue the process with the remaining sentences.

Intermediate

Part A: Follow the directions in Part A of the Beginning section, but substitute these questions:
• *Does the duck run or jump?*
• *Does a bug or a duck run?*

Part B: Tell students they will write words that name pictures. Then, help students identify the pictures. Have them complete the section with a partner.

Part C: Tell students they will choose words whose names have the short *u* sound to complete sentences. Say the word *up*, stressing the short *u* sound: /u/-/u/-/p/. Say the word again and have students repeat the word as they point to it. Then, repeat the process with the other words. Explain that all the words in the box have the short *u* sound. Next, read aloud the first sentence with the rebus. Pause to allow students time to write their answer. Continue the process with the remaining sentences.

Advanced

Part A: Distribute page 35. Direct students to look at the picture of the duck running. Read the sentence aloud and have students repeat it. Invite students to talk about the picture. Repeat the sentence, stressing the short *u* sound in each word: *The /d/-/u/-/u/-/k/ can /r/-/u/-/u/-/n/.* Tell students that *duck* and *run* have the short *u* sound. Point out that the words *duck* and *run* are in dark print.

Parts B and C: Read aloud the directions. Ask students to skim the page to see if they have a question about any of the words. Have students complete the page independently.

EXTENSION

Invite students to draw a picture of bugs jumping

Short *u*

A. Read the sentence.

The **duck** can **run**.

B. Write the name of each picture. Use the words in dark print above.

1.

_____

2.

_____

C. Write a word from the box to complete each sentence.

up	rug	bug

3. The duck can fly _____.

4. The duck eats a _____.

5. The duck is on the _____.

Long *a* (*a_e*)

NOTE: Students whose native language is French, Urdu, or Vietnamese may have problems with the long *a* sound.

INTRODUCTION

Take students outside and display a rake. Say: *This is a rake.* Have students repeat the sentence. Then, invite each student to rake as they say: *(Name) can rake.* Discuss that rake has two meanings, as a tool and as an action. After returning to the classroom, say *rake* again, stressing the middle sound: */r/-/ā/-/ā/-/k/.* Explain that /ā/ is the long *a* sound.

 Some students may hear /a/ or /e/ in words having the long *a* sound.

Beginning

Part A: Distribute page 37. Direct students to look at the first picture. Read the sentence aloud and have students repeat it. Invite each student to act out the sentence as they repeat it. Then, ask the following questions about the picture:
• *What is Jane next to? Point to it.*
• *What will Jane do? Show me.*

Repeat the sentence, stressing the long *a* sound in each word: */j/-/ā/-/ā/-/n/ will /r/-/ā/-/ā/-/k/ by the /g/-/ā/-/ā/-/t/.* Tell students that *Jane, rake,* and *gate* all have the long *a* sound. Explain that the final *e* is silent and changes the vowel so that it says its name. Point out that the words *rake* and *gate* are in dark print.

Part B: Tell students they will write words that name pictures. Have students point to the rake and say the picture name. Then, have students point to the words in dark print in the sentence above. Ask questions that help students choose and write the word *rake.* Repeat with the picture of the gate.

Part C: Tell students that they will circle sentences that tell about pictures. Explain that the pictures show students doing something in which the name has a long *a* sound. Remind students of the *a_e* vowel pattern. Then, have students look at the first picture. Read aloud the sentences, pausing to let students repeat each one. Ask questions that help students choose and circle the correct sentence. Continue the process with the remaining pictures and sentences.

Intermediate

Part A: Follow the directions in Part A of the Beginning section, but substitute these questions:
• *What is Jane next to?*
• *What will Jane do?*

Part B: Tell students they will write words that name pictures. Then, help students identify the pictures. Have them complete the section with a partner.

Part C: Tell students that they will circle sentences that tell about pictures. Explain that the pictures show students doing something in which the name has a long *a* sound. Remind students of the *a_e* vowel pattern. Then, have students look at the first picture. Read aloud the sentences, pausing before saying the last word with the *a_e* vowel pattern. Challenge students to silently read the words and circle their answer. Continue the process with the remaining pictures and sentences.

Advanced

Part A: Distribute page 37. Direct students to look at the first picture. Read the sentence aloud and have students repeat it. Invite students to talk about the picture. Repeat the sentence, stressing the long *a* sound in each word: */j/-/ā/-/ā/-/n/ will /r/-/ā/-/ā/-/k/ by the /g/-/ā/-/ā/-/t/.* Tell students that *Jane, rake,* and *gate* all have the long *a* sound. Explain that the final *e* is silent and changes the vowel so that it says its name. Point out that the words *rake* and *gate* are in dark print.

Parts B and C: Read aloud the directions. Ask students to skim the page to see if they have a question about any of the words. Have students complete the page independently.

EXTENSION

Remind students that *game* follows the *a_e* pattern. Allow students to play games.

Name _____   Date _____

Long *a* (*a_e*)

A. Read the sentence.

Jane   will   **rake**   by   the   **gate**.

B. Write the name of each picture. Use the words in dark print above.

1.

_____

2.

_____

C. Read each sentence. Circle the sentence that matches the picture.

3. The students play a game.

The students wave.

4. The students eat grapes.

The students made a cake.

5. The students are at the lake.

The students see a snake.

Long *a* (*ay* and *ai*)

NOTE: Students whose native language is French, Urdu, or Vietnamese may have problems with the long *a* sound.

INTRODUCTION

Provide a handful of hay. Say: *This is hay.* Have students repeat the sentence. Say *hay* again, stressing the ending sound: /h/-/ā/-/ā/. Remind students that /ā/ is the long *a* sound. Explain that the long *a* sound has several spelling patterns. Write *hay, rain,* and *rake* on the board and underline the long *a* spelling pattern in each. Say the words as you point to them and have students repeat the words. Discuss the differences in the spelling patterns. Tell students that they will learn words that have the *ai* and *ay* patterns.

 Invite students to say the word *hay* in their native language and tell what kinds of animals eat hay.

 The homograph *train* may confuse students. Explain that *train* has two meanings. Say simple sentences that provide context clues of the word's use. (*The train rolls on a track. People train in a sport to become better.*)

Beginning

Part A: Distribute page 39. Direct students to look at the first picture. Read the sentence aloud and have students repeat it. Pass the hay to each student and invite the student to repeat the sentence. Then, ask the following questions about the picture:
• *Where is the quail? Point to it.*
• *What is sleeping in the hay? Point to it.*

Repeat the sentence, stressing the long *a* sound in each word: *The /kw/-/ā/-/ā/-/l/ is in the /h/-/ā/-/ā/.* Tell students that *quail* and *hay* have the long *a* sound. Remind students of the different spelling patterns for long *a*. Point out that the words *quail* and *hay* are in dark print.

Part B: Tell students they will write words that name pictures. Have students point to the quail and say the picture name. Then, have students point to the words in dark print in the sentence above. Ask questions that help students choose and write the word *quail*. Repeat with the picture of the hay.

Part C: Tell students they will choose words whose names have the long *a* sound to complete sentences. Read aloud the first sentence with the rebus. Say *rain* again, stressing the long *a* sound: /r/-/ā/-/ā/-/n/. Remind students of the different vowel patterns for long *a*. Then, say *rain* again for them to repeat. Tell students that *rain* is spelled *r, a, i, n.* Help them find the word in the list, write it on the line, and cross out the word once it is chosen. Continue the process with the remaining sentences.

Intermediate

Part A: Follow the directions in Part A of the Beginning section, but substitute these questions:
• *Where is the quail?*
• *What is sleeping in the hay?*

Part B: Tell students they will write words that name pictures. Then, help students identify the pictures. Have them complete the section with a partner.

Part C: Tell students they will choose words whose names have the long *a* sound to complete sentences. Say the word *train*, stressing the long *a* sound /tr/-/ā/-/ā/-/n/. Say the word again and have students repeat the word as they point to it. Then, repeat the process with the other words. Explain that all the words in the box have the long *a* sound. Next, read aloud the first sentence with the rebus. Pause to allow students time to write their answer. Continue the process with the remaining sentences.

Advanced

Part A: Distribute page 39. Direct students to look at the first picture. Read the sentence aloud and have students repeat it. Invite students to talk about the picture. Repeat the sentence, stressing the long *a* sound in each word: *The /kw/-/ā/-/ā/-/l/ is in the /h/-/ā/-/ā/.* Tell students that *quail* and *hay* have the long *a* sound. Remind students of the different spelling patterns for long *a*. Point out that the words *quail* and *hay* are in dark print.

Parts B and C: Read aloud the directions. Ask students to skim the page to see if they have a question about any of the words. Have students complete the page independently.

EXTENSION

Tell students that a long time ago students played a game called *jackstraws*. The game *pick-up sticks* is based on the old game. Explain that the word *hay* is another word for *straw*. Then, drop a handful of hay. Invite students to pick up a piece of hay without moving other pieces.

Name _____   Date _____

Long *a* (*ay* and *ai*)

A. Read the sentence.

    The **quail** is in the **hay**.

B. Write the name of each picture. Use the words in dark print above.

1.

_____

2.

_____

C. Write a word from the box to complete each sentence.

train   tray   rain

3. The quail is in the _____.

4. A _____ goes fast.

5. The food is on the _____.

Long e (ee and ea)

NOTE: Students whose native language is French, Greek, Urdu, or Vietnamese may have problems with the long *e* sound.

INTRODUCTION

Display a leaf. Say: *This is a leaf.* Have students repeat the sentence. Say *leaf* again, stressing the middle sound: /l/-/ē/-/ē/-/f/. Remind students that /ē/ is the long *e* sound. Explain that the long *e* sound has several spelling patterns. Write *leaf* and *bee* on the board and underline the long *e* spelling pattern in each. Say the words as you point to them and have students repeat the words. Discuss the differences in the spelling patterns. Tell students that they will learn words that have the *ee* and *ea* patterns for long *e*.

 Invite students to say the word *leaf* in their native language.

 Students may confuse the words *leaf* and *leave* because of the final consonant sounds. Write the words on the board and pronounce them slowly, stressing the ending sound. Use the words in context and have students point to the word used in each sentence.

Beginning

Part A: Distribute page 41. Direct students to look at the first picture. Read the sentence aloud and have students repeat it. Then, pass a leaf to each student and invite the student to repeat the sentence individually. Next, ask the following questions about the picture:
• *Where is the bee? Point to it.*
• *What is on the leaf? Point to it.*

Repeat the sentence, stressing the long *e* sound in each word: *The /b/-/ē/-/ē/ is on the /l/-/ē/-/ē/-/f/.* Tell students that *bee* and *leaf* have the long *e* sound. Remind students of the different spelling patterns for long *e*. Point out that the words *bee* and *leaf* are in dark print.

Part B: Tell students they will write words that name pictures. Have students point to the bee and say the picture name. Then, have students point to the words in dark print in the sentence above. Ask questions that help students choose and write the word *bee*. Repeat with the picture of the leaf.

Part C: Tell students that they will circle sentences that tell about pictures. Explain that the pictures show something that has the long *e* sound. Remind students of the different vowel patterns for long *e*. Then, have students look at the first picture. Read aloud the sentences, pausing to let students repeat each one. Ask questions that help students choose and circle the correct sentence. Continue the process with the remaining pictures and sentences.

Intermediate

Part A: Follow the directions in Part A of the Beginning section, but substitute these questions:
• *What is on the leaf?*
• *Where is the bee?*

Part B: Tell students they will write words that name pictures. Then, help students identify the pictures. Have them complete the section with a partner.

Part C: Tell students that they will circle sentences that tell about pictures. Explain that the pictures show something that has the long *e* sound. Remind students of the different vowel patterns for long *e*. Then, have students look at the first picture. Read aloud the sentences, omitting the word that identifies the correct sentence. Challenge students to silently read those words and circle their answer. Continue the process with the remaining pictures and sentences.

Advanced

Part A: Distribute page 41. Direct students to look at the first picture. Read the sentence aloud and have students repeat it. Invite students to talk about the picture. Repeat the sentence, stressing the long *e* sound in each word: *The /b/-/ē/-/ē/ is on the /l/-/ē/-/ē/-/f/.* Tell students that *bee* and *leaf* have the long *e* sound. Remind students of the different spelling patterns for long *e*. Point out that the words *bee* and *leaf* are in dark print.

Parts B and C: Read aloud the directions. Ask students to skim the page to see if they have a question about any of the words. Have students complete the page independently.

EXTENSION

Gather leaves of different shapes. Invite students to trace them. Then, challenge students to write words that contain the long *e* sound on the leaves.

Name _____   Date _____

Long *e* (*ee* and *ea*)

A. Read the sentence.

The **bee** is on the **leaf**.

B. Write the name of each picture. Use the words in dark print above.

1.

2.

_____   _____

C. Read each sentence. Circle the sentence that matches the picture.

3. The bee sits on a weed.

   The bee sits on a tree.

4. The sheep eat.

   The sheep sleep.

5. We wear shoes in the sea.

   We wear shoes on our feet.

Long *i* (*i_e* and *ie*)

INTRODUCTION

Write a numeral five on the board. Say: *This is a five.* Have students repeat the sentence. Invite each student to find a group of five items, such as crayons or books. Have them repeat the sentence, saying *This is five (items named).* Say *five,* stressing the long *i* sound: /f/-/ī/-/ī/-/v/. Explain that /ī/ is the long *i* sound. Explain that the long *i* sound has several spelling patterns. Write *pie* on the board beside *five* and underline the long *i* spelling pattern in each. Say the words as you point to them and have students repeat the words. Discuss the differences in the spelling patterns. Tell students that they will learn words that have the *i_e* and *ie* patterns.

 Invite students to count the five items in their native language.

 Some students may hear /a/ in words having the long *i* sound.

Beginning

Part A: Distribute page 43. Direct students to look at the picture of the five pies. Read the sentence aloud and have students repeat it. Ask five students to read the sentence together. Then, ask the following questions about the picture:
• *What did Mike make? Point to them.*
• *How many pies did Mike make? Point to them as we count them together.*

Repeat the sentence, stressing the long *i* sound in each word: /m/-/ī/-/ī/-/k/ made /f/-/ī/-/ī/-/v/ /p/-/ī/-/ī/-/z/. Tell students that *Mike, five,* and *pies* have the long *i* sound. Remind students of the different spelling patterns for long *i*. Point out that the words *five* and *pies* are in dark print.

Part B: Tell students they will write words that name pictures. Have students point to the five and say the picture name. Then, have students point to the words in dark print in the sentence above. Ask questions that help students choose and write the word *five*. Repeat with the picture of the pies.

Part C: Tell students they will choose words whose names have the long *i* sound to complete sentences. Read aloud the first sentence with the rebus. Say *bike* again, stressing the long *i* sound: /b/-/ī/-/ī/-/k/. Remind students of the different vowel patterns for long *i*. Then, say *bike* again for them to repeat. Tell students that *bike* is spelled *b,*

i, k, e. Help them find the word in the list, write it on the line, and cross out the word once it is chosen. Continue the process with the remaining sentences.

Intermediate

Part A: Follow the directions in Part A of the Beginning section, but substitute these questions:
• *What did Mike make?*
• *How many pies did Mike make?*

Part B: Tell students they will write words that name pictures. Then, help students identify the pictures. Have them complete the section with a partner.

Part C: Tell students they will choose words whose names have the long *i* sound to complete sentences. Say the word *bike*, stressing the long *i* sound: /b/-/ī/-/ī/-/k/. Say the word again and have students repeat the word as they point to it. Then, repeat the process with the other words. Explain that all the words in the box have the long *i* sound. Next, remind students of the different vowel patterns for long *i*. Next, read aloud the first sentence with the rebus. Pause to allow students time to write their answer. Continue the process with the remaining sentences.

Advanced

Part A: Distribute page 43. Direct students to look at the picture of the five pies. Read the sentence aloud and have students repeat it. Invite students to talk about the picture. Repeat the sentence, stressing the long *i* sound in each word: /m/-/ī/-/ī/-/k/ made /f/-/ī/-/ī/-/v/ /p/-/ī/-/ī/-/z/. Tell students that *Mike, five,* and *pies* have the long *i* sound. Remind students of the different spelling patterns for long *i*. Point out that the words *five* and *pies* are in dark print.

Parts B and C: Read aloud the directions. Ask students to skim the page to see if they have a question about any of the words. Have students complete the page independently.

EXTENSION

Write the words *white* and *write* on the board. Point out that both words have the *i_e* vowel pattern. Invite students to write in white chalk other words that have the long *i* vowel patterns on black paper.

Long o (*oa* and *oe*)

A. Read the sentence.

 The **doe** is by the **road**.

B. Write the name of each picture. Use the words in dark print above.

1.

_____

2.

_____

C. Read each sentence. Circle the sentence that matches the picture.

3. The doe saw a boat.

The doe saw a toad.

4. The man has a hoe.

The man has soap.

5. The girl wears a coat.

The girl hurt her toe.

Long *u* (u_e)

NOTE: Students whose native language is Chinese or Korean may have problems with the long *u* sound.

INTRODUCTION

Display a picture of a flute. Say: *This is a flute.* Have students repeat the sentence. Pass the picture to each student and say: *(Name) is holding the flute.* Encourage the students to repeat the sentence each time. Say *flute* again, stressing the long *u* sound: /fl/-/ū/-/ū/-/t/. Explain that /ū/ is the long *u* sound.

 Invite students to name and describe an instrument in their native country that looks like or is played like a flute.

Beginning

Part A: Distribute page 49. Direct students to look at the picture of the girl playing the flute. Read the sentence aloud and have students repeat it. Then, invite each student to hold the picture of the flute and to repeat the sentence individually. Ask the following questions about the picture:
• *Who plays the flute? Point to it.*
• *What is June playing? Point to it.*
• *Is the flute playing a tune?*

Repeat the sentence, stressing the long *u* sound in each word: /j/-/ū/-/ū/-/n/ *plays a* /t/-/ū/-/ū/-/n/ *on her* /fl/-/ū/-/ū/-/t/. Tell students that *June, tune,* and *flute* all have the long *u* sound. Explain that the final *e* is silent and changes the vowel so that it says its name. Point out that the words *tune* and *flute* are in dark print.

Part B: Tell students they will write words that name pictures. Have students point to the flute and say the picture name. Then, have students point to the words in dark print in the sentence above. Ask questions that help students choose and write the word *flute.* Repeat with the picture of the tune.

Part C: Tell students they will choose words whose names have the long *u* sound to complete sentences. Read aloud the first sentence with the rebus. Say *tube* again, stressing the long *u* sound: /t/-/ū/-/ū/-/b/. Remind students of the u_e vowel pattern. Tell students that *tube* is spelled *t, u, b, e.* Help them find the word in the list, write it on the line, and cross out the word once it is chosen. Continue the process with the remaining sentences.

Intermediate

Part A: Follow the directions in Part A of the Beginning section, but substitute these questions:
• *Who plays the flute?*
• *What is June playing?*
• *Is the flute playing a tune or cube?*

Part B: Tell students they will write words that name pictures. Then, help students identify the pictures. Have them complete the section with a partner.

Part C: Tell students they will choose words whose names have the long *u* sound to complete sentences. Say the word *tube,* stressing the long *u* sound: /t/-/ū/-/ū/-/b/. Say the word again and have students repeat the word as they point to it. Then, repeat the process with the other words. Explain that all the words in the box have the long *u* sound. Then, remind students of the u_e vowel pattern for long *u*. Next, read aloud the first sentence with the rebus. Pause to allow students time to write their answer. Continue the process with the remaining sentences.

Advanced

Part A: Distribute page 49. Direct students to look at the first picture. Read the sentence aloud and have students repeat it. Invite students to talk about the picture. Repeat the sentence, stressing the long *u* sound in each word: /j/-/ū/-/ū/-/n/ *plays a* /t/-/ū/-/ū/-/n/ *on her* /fl/-/ū/-/ū/-/t/. Tell students that *June, tune,* and *flute* all have the long *u* sound. Explain that the final *e* is silent and changes the vowel so that it says its name. Point out that the words *tune* and *flute* are in dark print.

Parts B and C: Read aloud the directions. Ask students to skim the page to see if they have a question about any of the words. Have students complete the page independently.

EXTENSION

Invite students to write words that have the long *u* sound on dark paper. Give them a cube of ice and tell them that *cube* has the long *u* sound. Invite them to rub the melting cube over the words to make word designs.

Long *u* (*u_e*)

A. Read the sentence.

 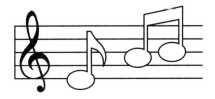

June plays a **tune** on her **flute**.

B. Write the name of each picture. Use the words in dark print above .

1.

_____

2.

_____

C. Write a word from the box to complete each sentence.

tube   mule   glue

3. June gets a _____ of paint.

4. June uses _____ on her picture.

5. June sees a cute baby _____.

y as a Vowel

NOTE: Students whose native language is French, Greek, Urdu, or Vietnamese may have problems with the long *e* sound.

INTRODUCTION
Draw a picture of a fly with a huge smile on the board. Then, write this sentence: *The fly is happy.* Read it out loud and have students repeat it. Invite students to draw their own pictures of flies and to repeat the sentence. Point out that the words *fly* and *happy* both end in the letter *y*. Explain that *y* stands for the long *i* sound in one-syllable words and the long *e* sound in multiple-syllable words.

 Invite students to share the word *fly* in their native language.

 The homograph *fly* may confuse students. Explain that *fly* has two meanings and define them. Then, say simple sentences that provide context clues of the word's use. *(Jan will fly on an airplane. A fly is a bug with wings.)* Invite students to clap when they hear a sentence in which *fly* refers to an insect.

Beginning
Part A: Distribute page 51. Direct students to look at the first picture. Read the sentence aloud and have students repeat it. Then, invite pairs of students to act out the scene and repeat the sentence when they are done. Next, ask the following questions about the picture:
• *What is chasing the fly? Point to it.*
• *What is moving away from the puppy? Point to it.*

Repeat the sentence, stressing the vowel sound *y* makes in each word: *The /pup/-/ē/-/ē/ ran after the /fl/-/ī/-/ī/.* Tell students that the *y* in *puppy* has the long *e* sound, and the *y* in *fly* has the long *i* sound. Point out that the words *puppy* and *fly* are in dark print.

Part B: Tell students they will write words that name pictures. Have students point to the fly and say the picture name. Then, have students point to the words in dark print in the sentence above. Ask questions that help students choose and write the word *fly*. Repeat with the picture of the puppy.

Part C: Tell students that they will circle sentences that tell about pictures. Explain that the pictures show something that has the sound of /ē/ or /ī/ spelled *y*. Then, have students look at the first

picture. Read aloud the sentences, pausing to let students repeat each one. Ask questions that help students choose and circle the correct sentence. Continue the process with the remaining pictures and sentences.

Intermediate
Part A: Follow the directions in Part A of the Beginning section, but substitute these questions:
• *What is running after the fly?*
• *What is the puppy chasing?*

Part B: Tell students they will write words that name pictures. Then, help students identify the pictures. Have them complete the section with a partner.

Part C: Tell students that they will circle sentences that tell about pictures. Explain that the pictures show something that has the sound of /ē/ or /ī/ spelled *y*. Then, have students look at the first picture. Read aloud the sentences, omitting the word that identifies the correct sentence. Challenge students to silently read those words and circle their answer. Continue the process with the remaining pictures and sentences.

Advanced
Part A: Distribute page 51. Direct students to look at the first picture. Read the sentence aloud and have students repeat it. Invite students to talk about the picture. Repeat the sentence, stressing the vowel sound *y* makes in each word: *The /pup/-/ē/-/ē/ ran after the /fl/-/ī/-/ī/.* Tell students that the *y* in *puppy* has the long *e* sound, and the *y* in *fly* has the long *i* sound. Point out that the words *puppy* and *fly* are in dark print.

Parts B and C: Read aloud the directions. Ask students to skim the page to see if they have a question about any of the words. Have students complete the page independently.

EXTENSION
Write the following words on cards: *cry, fry, sky, city, story, body.* Display each card and read the word out loud. Have students repeat the words and tell which ending sound *y* makes.

y as a Vowel

A. Read the sentence.

 The **puppy** ran after the **fly**.

B. Write the name of each picture. Use the words in dark print above.

1.

2.

_____   _____

C. Read each sentence. Circle the sentence that matches the picture.

3. The puppy is in the country.

The puppy is in the city.

4. The baby is happy.

The baby did cry.

5. The sun is in the sky.

The bunny is in the sky.

r-Controlled Vowel *ar*

NOTE: Students whose native language is Italian may have problems with the *ar* sound.

INTRODUCTION

Display a small model car. Say: *This is a car.* Have students repeat the sentence. Pass the car to each student and say: *(Name) is holding the car.* Encourage the students to repeat the sentence each time. Say *car* again, stressing the ending sound: */k/-/är/-/är/.* Tell students that /är/ is made with the letters *a* and *r.*

 Invite students to say the word *car* in their native language.

Beginning

Part A: Distribute page 53. Direct students to look at the first picture. Read the sentence aloud and have students repeat it. Then, pass a car to each student and invite the student to repeat the sentence individually. Next, ask the following questions about the picture:
• *Where is the car? Point to it.*
• *What is by the barn? Point to it.*

Repeat the sentence, stressing the *ar* sound in each word: *The /k/-/är/-/är/ is by the /b/-/är/-/är/-/n/.* Tell students that *car* and *barn* have the *ar* sound. Point out that the words *car* and *barn* are in dark print.

Part B: Tell students they will write words that name pictures. Have students point to the barn and say the picture name. Then, have students point to the words in dark print in the sentence above. Ask questions that help students choose and write the word *barn.* Repeat with the picture of the car.

Part C: Tell students that they will circle sentences that tell about pictures. Explain that the pictures show something that has the *ar* sound. Then, have students look at the first picture. Read aloud the sentences, pausing to let students repeat each one. Ask questions that help students choose and circle the correct sentence. Continue the process with the remaining pictures and sentences.

Intermediate

Part A: Follow the directions in Part A of the Beginning section, but substitute these questions:
• *What is by the barn?*
• *Where is the car?*

Part B: Tell students they will write words that name pictures. Then, help students identify the pictures. Have them complete the section with a partner.

Part C: Tell students that they will circle sentences that tell about pictures. Explain that the pictures show something that has the *ar* sound. Then, have students look at the first picture. Read aloud the sentences, omitting the word that identifies the correct sentence. Challenge students to silently read those words and circle their answer. Continue the process with the remaining pictures and sentences.

Advanced

Part A: Distribute page 53. Direct students to look at the first picture. Read the sentence aloud and have students repeat it. Invite students to talk about the picture. Repeat the sentence, stressing the *ar* sound in each word: *The /k/-/är/-/är/ is by the /b/-/är/-/är/-/n/.* Tell students that *barn* and *car* have the *ar* sound. Point out that the words *car* and *barn* are in dark print.

Parts B and C: Read aloud the directions. Ask students to skim the page to see if they have a question about any of the words. Have students complete the page independently.

EXTENSION

Invite students to cut out stars from yellow construction paper. Remind them that *star* has the *ar* sound. Then, challenge students to write words that contain the *ar* sound on the stars.

r-Controlled Vowel *ar*

A. Read the sentence.

 The **car** is by the **barn**.

B. Write the name of each picture. Use the words in dark print above.

1.

_____

2.

_____

C. Read each sentence. Circle the sentence that matches the picture.

3. The car has a star.

The car is far away.

4. I hear a harp.

I see the art.

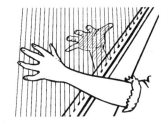

5. Grandma has yarn.

Grandma has a dart.

r-Controlled Vowel *or*

INTRODUCTION

Display a can of corn or an ear of corn. Say: *This is corn.* Have students repeat the sentence. Pass the corn to each student and say *(Name) is holding the corn.* Encourage the students to repeat the sentence each time. Say *corn* again, stressing the *or* sound: */k/-/ôr/-/ôr/-/n/.* Tell students that /ôr/ is made with the letters *o* and *r.*

 Invite students to share the word *corn* in their native language and tell their favorite way to eat it.

Beginning

Part A: Distribute page 55. Direct students to look at the picture of the horse eating corn. Read the sentence aloud and have students repeat it. Then, invite each student to hold the corn and to repeat the sentence individually. Ask the following questions about the picture:
• *Who eats corn? Point to it.*
• *What is the horse eating? Point to it.*

Repeat the sentence, stressing the *or* sound in each word: *The /h/-/ôr/-/ôr/-/s/ eats /k/-/ôr/-/ôr/-/n/.* Tell students that *horse* and *corn* have the *or* sound. Point out that the words *horse* and *corn* are in dark print.

Part B: Tell students they will write words that name pictures. Have students point to the horse and say the picture name. Then, have students point to the words in dark print in the sentence above. Ask questions that help students choose and write the word *horse.* Repeat with the picture of the corn.

Part C: Tell students they will underline words that have the *or* sound and then draw lines to match each sentence with a picture. Then, read aloud the first sentence. Write *or* on the board and remind students that the letters *o* and *r* together stand for the *or* sound. Guide students to look for the word with *or* and to underline it. Say *porch,* stressing the *or* sound: */p/-/ôr/-/ôr/-/ch/.* Next, ask questions that help students name and draw a line to the picture of the porch. Continue the process with the remaining sentences and pictures.

Intermediate

Part A: Follow the directions in Part A of the Beginning section, but substitute these questions:
• *Who eats corn?*
• *What is the horse eating?*

Part B: Tell students they will write words that name pictures. Then, help students identify the pictures. Have them complete the section with a partner.

Part C: Tell students they will underline words that have the *or* sound and then draw lines to match each sentence with a picture. Have students point to each picture as you discuss it, stressing the *or* sound. Have them repeat it. Then, read aloud each sentence. Pause as students underline the word that has *or* and draw a line from the sentence to the corresponding picture.

Advanced

Part A: Distribute page 55. Direct students to look at the picture of the horse eating corn. Read the sentence aloud and have students repeat it. Invite students to talk about the picture. Repeat the sentence, stressing the *or* sound in each word: *The /h/-/ôr/-/ôr/-/s/ eats /k/-/ôr/-/ôr/-/n/.* Tell students that *horse* and *corn* have the *or* sound. Point out that the words *horse* and *corn* are in dark print.

Parts B and C: Read aloud the directions. Ask students to skim the page to see if they have a question about any of the words. Have students complete the page independently.

EXTENSION

Duplicate several pages from a catalog and the order form. Write *order* on the board and explain what an order form is. Point out that the word has the *or* sound. Invite students to practice filling out the form using the duplicated pages of the catalog.

r-Controlled Vowel *or*

A. Read the sentence.

 The **horse** eats **corn**.

B. Write the name of each picture. Use the words in dark print above.

1.

_____

2.

_____

C. Underline the word that has *or*. Then, draw lines to match the sentence with its picture.

a.

3. A bird is by the porch.

b.

4. The rose has a thorn.

5. Luis is at the store.

c.

r-Controlled Vowel *er, ir, ur*

INTRODUCTION

Display a picture of a bird. Say: *This is a bird.* Have students repeat the sentence. Say *bird* again, stressing the middle sound: */b/-/ûr/-/ûr/-/d/.* Tell students that /ûr/ is the *er* sound. Explain that the *er* sound has several spelling patterns. Write *bird, nurse,* and *fern* on the board and underline the *er* spelling pattern in each. Say the words as you point to them and have students repeat the words. Discuss the differences in the spelling patterns. Tell students that they will learn words that have the *er, ir,* and *ur* patterns.

 Invite students to say the word *bird* in their native language.

Beginning

Part A: Distribute page 57. Direct students to look at the first picture. Read the sentence aloud and have students repeat it. Then, invite each student to repeat the sentence individually. Next, ask the following questions about the picture:
• *What is in the fern? Point to it.*
• *Who is looking at the bird? Point to it.*
• *Where is the bird? Point to it.*

Repeat the sentence, stressing the *er* sound in each word: *The /n/-/ûr/-/ûr/-/s/ saw the /b/-/ûr/-/ûr/-/d/ in the /f/-/ûr/-/ûr/-/n/.* Tell students that *nurse, bird,* and *fern* all have the *er* sound. Remind students of the different spelling patterns for *er.* Point out that the words *nurse, bird,* and *fern* are in dark print.

Part B: Tell students they will write words that name pictures. Have students point to the fern and say the picture name. Then, have students point to the words in dark print in the sentence above. Ask questions that help students choose and write the word *fern.* Repeat with the pictures of the nurse and bird.

Part C: Tell students they will choose words whose names have the *er* sound to complete sentences. Read aloud the first sentence with the rebus. Say *purse* again, stressing the *er* sound: */p/-/ûr/-/ûr/-/s/.* Remind students that the spelling pattern *ur* stands for the *er* sound. Tell students that *purse* is spelled *p, u, r, s, e.* Help them find the word in the list, write it on the line, and cross out the word once it is chosen. Continue the process with the remaining sentences.

Intermediate

Part A: Follow the directions in Part A of the Beginning section, but substitute these questions:
• *Is the nurse or the bird in the fern?*
• *Is the bird on the nurse or in the fern?*
• *Who sees the bird?*

Part B: Tell students they will write words that name pictures. Then, help students identify the pictures. Have them complete the section with a partner.

Part C: Tell students they will choose words whose names have the *er* sound to complete sentences. Say the word *purse,* stressing the *er* sound: */p/-/ûr/-/ûr/-/s/.* Remind students that the spelling pattern *ur* stands for the *er* sound. Say the word again and have students repeat the word as they point to it. Then, repeat the process with the other words. Explain that all the words in the box have the *er* sound. Next, read aloud the first sentence with the rebus. Pause to allow students time to write their answer. Continue the process with the remaining sentences.

Advanced

Part A: Distribute page 57. Direct students to look at the first picture. Read the sentence aloud and have students repeat it. Invite students to talk about the picture. Repeat the sentence, stressing the *er* sound in each word: *The /n/-/ûr/-/ûr/-/s/ saw the /b/-/ûr/-/ûr/-/d/ in the /f/-/ûr/-/ûr/-/n/.* Tell students that *nurse, bird,* and *fern* all have the *er* sound. Remind students of the different spelling patterns for *er.* Point out that the words *nurse, bird,* and *fern* are in dark print.

Parts B and C: Read aloud the directions. Ask students to skim the page to see if they have a question about any of the words. Have students complete the page independently.

EXTENSION

Provide cutouts shaped like fern leaves to students. Challenge them to write words that have the *er* sound on them. Have students sort the leaves by the spelling patterns and then arrange the leaves with the same spelling patterns on a branch to form a fern.

r-Controlled Vowels *er, ir, ur*

A. Read the sentence.

 The **nurse** saw the **bird** in the **fern**.

B. Write the name of each picture. Use the words in dark print above.

1.

2.

3.

_____ _____ _____

C. Write a word from the box to complete each sentence.

| purse   shirt   person |

4. The nurse buys a _____.

5. The nurse is a _____.

6. The nurse buys a _____.

Vowel Digraph *ea*

NOTE: Students whose native language is Urdu may have problems with the short *e* sound. Students whose native language is French, Greek, Urdu, or Vietnamese may have problems with the long *e* sound.

INTRODUCTION

Display a loaf of bread. Say: *This is bread.* Have students repeat the sentence. Pass the bread around and invite students to take a slice to eat. Write *bread* on the board and underline the digraph *ea*. Next, write *tea* on the board, say it, and underline the digraph *ea*. Explain that when the letters *e* and *a* are together, they can stand for two sounds—the short *e* sound as in *bread* and the long *e* sound as in *tea*.

 Explain that bread is a food served during many American meals. Invite students to share foods that are served in their cultural meals.

Beginning

Part A: Distribute page 59. Direct students to look at the picture of the girl eating bread. Read the sentence aloud and have students repeat it. Then, invite each student to say the sentence individually. Ask the following questions about the picture:
• *Is the girl eating bread? Point to it.*
• *Is the girl drinking tea? Point to it.*

Repeat the sentence, stressing the sounds for the digraph *ea* in each word: *The girl had /br/-/e/-/e/-/d/ and /t/-/ē/-/ē/.* Remind students that *bread* has the short *e* sound and *tea* has the long *e* sound. Point out that the words *bread* and *tea* are in dark print.

Part B: Tell students they will write words that name pictures. Have students point to the tea and say the picture name. Then, have students point to the words in dark print in the sentence above. Ask questions that help students choose and write the word *tea*. Repeat with the picture of the bread.

Part C: Tell students they will write words for pictures whose names have the digraph *ea*. Review the vowel sounds for the digraph *ea*. Then, identify the picture of the team. Have students repeat the word. Say the picture name again, stressing the long *e* sound: */t/-/ē/-/ē/-/m/.* Have students tell if they hear a long or short *e* sound. Next, tell students that *team* is spelled *t, e, a, m.* Help them find the word in the list, write it on the line, and cross out the word once it is chosen. Continue the process with the remaining pictures by identifying

the picture, the vowel sound, and the spelling of the name. When the students are done, have them circle the pictures in which the digraph *ea* stands for the short *e* sound.

Intermediate

Part A: Follow the directions in Part A of the Beginning section, but substitute these questions:
• *Is the girl eating bread or a peach?*
• *Is the girl drinking tea or milk?*

Part B: Tell students they will write words that name pictures. Then, help students identify the pictures. Have them complete the section with a partner.

Part C: Tell students they will write words for pictures whose names have the digraph *ea*. Review the vowel sounds for the digraph *ea*. Then, identify the picture of the team. Have students repeat the word. Say the picture name again, stressing the long *e* sound: */t/-/ē/-/ē/-/m/.* Have students tell whether they hear a long or short *e* sound. Next, tell students that *team* is spelled *t, e, a, m.* Help them find the word in the list, write it on the line, and cross out the word once it is chosen. Help students identify the names of the remaining pictures. Ask students to work with a partner to complete the page.

Advanced

Part A: Distribute page 59. Direct students to look at the picture of the girl eating bread. Read the sentence aloud and have students repeat it. Invite students to talk about the picture. Repeat the sentence, stressing the sounds for the digraph *ea* in each word: *The girl had /br/-/e/-/e/-/d/ and /t/-/ē/-/ē/.* Remind students that *bread* has the short *e* sound and *tea* has the long *e* sound. Point out that the words *bread* and *tea* are in dark print.

Parts B and C: Read aloud the directions. Ask students to skim the page to see if they have a question about any of the words. Have students complete the page independently.

EXTENSION

Write these sentences on the board: *I like to read. I read a book yesterday.* Read aloud the sentences and underline *read* in each. Have students tell what sound the digraph *ea* stands for. Lead students in a discussion explaining that they will need to use context clues to find out how the word is pronounced.

Name _____ Date _____

Vowel Digraph *ea*

A. Read the sentence.

   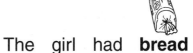

The girl had **bread** and **tea**.

B. Write the name of each picture. Use the words in dark print above.

1.

2.

_____ _____

C. Write the word that names the picture. Then, circle the pictures whose names have the short *e* sound.

| peach | sweater | head | jeans | thread | team |

3.    4.    5.

_____ _____ _____

6.    7.    8.

_____ _____ _____

Vowel Digraphs *au, aw, al, all*

NOTE: Students whose native language is Greek may have problems with the *aw* sound.

INTRODUCTION

Pantomime a yawn. Say: *This is a yawn.* Have students repeat the sentence. Encourage students to repeat the sentence as they pantomime a yawn. Repeat the process by pantomiming a walk. Next, write *yawn* and *walk* on the board. Underline the letters in each word that stand for the *aw* sound. Explain that the *aw* sound has several spelling patterns. Then, write *hall* and *sauce* on the board. Say the words and have students repeat them. Briefly explain their meanings. Next, underline the letters that stand for the *aw* sound. Point out that *au, aw, al,* and *all* can stand for the *aw* sound.

 Invite students to say and explain the meanings of words in their native language that have the *aw* sound.

 Some students may hear /o/ in words having the *aw* sound.

Beginning

Part A: Distribute page 61. Direct students to look at the first picture. Read the sentence aloud and have students repeat it. Then, invite each student to say the sentence individually as they pantomime it. Ask the following questions about the picture:
• *Where is the girl? Point to it.*
• *What is the girl doing while she walks? Show me.*
• *Is the girl walking?*
• *Is the girl running?*

Repeat the sentence, stressing the *aw* sound in each word: *The girl /y/-/aw/-/aw/-/nz/ as she /w/-/aw/-/aw/-/lks/ down the /h/-/aw/-/aw/-/l/.* Tell students that *yawns, walks,* and *hall* have the *aw* sound. Remind students of the different spelling patterns for *aw*. Point out that the words *yawns, walks,* and *hall* are in dark print.

Part B: Tell students they will write words that name pictures. Have students point to the hall and say the picture name. Then, have students point to the words in dark print in the sentence above. Ask questions that help students choose and write the word *hall*. Repeat with the other pictures.

Part C: Direct students' attention to the board and remind them of the other letter pairs that stand for the *aw* sound. Tell students they will write words for pictures whose names have the *aw* sound. Then, identify the picture of the saucer. Have

students repeat the word. Say the picture name again, stressing the *aw* sound: */s/-/aw/-/aw/-/sûr/.* Tell students that *saucer* is spelled *s, a, u, c, e, r.* Help them find the word in the list, write it on the line, and cross out the word once it is chosen. Continue the process with the remaining pictures. When the students are done, have them circle the letter pairs that stand for the *aw* sound.

Intermediate

Part A: Follow the directions in Part A of the Beginning section.

Part B: Tell students they will write words that name pictures. Then, help students identify the pictures. Have them complete the section with a partner.

Part C: Direct students' attention to the board and remind them of the other letter pairs that stand for the *aw* sound. Tell students they will write words for pictures whose names have the *aw* sound. Then, identify the picture of the saucer. Have students repeat the word. Say the picture name again, stressing the *aw* sound: */s/-/aw/-/aw/-/sûr/.* Tell students that *saucer* is spelled *s, a, u, c, e, r.* Help them find the word in the list, write it on the line, and cross out the word once it is chosen. Help students identify the names of the remaining pictures. Ask students to work with a partner to complete the page.

Advanced

Part A: Distribute page 61. Direct students to look at the first picture. Read the sentence aloud and have students repeat it. Invite students to talk about the picture. Repeat the sentence, stressing the *aw* sound in each word: *The girl /y/-/aw/-/aw/-/nz/ as she /w/-/aw/-/aw/-/lks/ down the /h/-/aw/-/aw/-/l/.* Tell students that *yawns, walks,* and *hall* have the *aw* sound. Remind students of the different spelling patterns for *aw*. Point out that the words *yawns, walks,* and *hall* are in dark print.

Parts B and C: Read aloud the directions. Ask students to skim the page to see if they have a question about any of the words. Have students complete the page independently.

EXTENSION

Write words with the *aw* sound on cards. Have students say the words and sort them into groups by the spelling patterns.

Vowel Digraphs *au*, *aw*, *al*, *all*

A. Read the sentence.

The girl **yawns** as she **walks** down the **hall**.

B. Write the name of each picture. Use the words in dark print above.

1.

2.

3.

_____   _____   _____

C. Write the word that names the picture. Then, circle the letters that stand for the *aw* sound.

| ball   saucer   paw   talk   chalk   faucet |

4.

5.

6.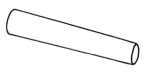

_____   _____   _____

7.

8.

9.

_____   _____   _____

Diphthong *ow*

INTRODUCTION

Write *town* on the board and say it. Have students repeat the word. Name things that are found in a town, such as stores and parks. Next, write *snow* on the board. Say it and have students repeat it. Underline the diphthong *ow* in each word. Explain that when the letters *o* and *w* are together, they can stand for two sounds—the *ow* sound as in *town*, and the long *o* sound as in *snow*.

 Invite students to share the word *town* in their native language.

Beginning

Part A: Distribute page 63. Direct students to look at the first picture. Read the sentence aloud and have students repeat it. Then, invite each student to say the sentence individually. Ask the following questions about the picture:
• *Does the picture show a town? Point to it.*
• *Does the picture show rain?*
• *Does the picture show snow?*

Repeat the sentence, stressing the sounds for the diphthong *ow* in each word: *The /sn/-/ō/-/ō/ fell on the /t/-/ow/-/ow/-/n/*. Remind students that *snow* has the long *o* sound and *town* has the *ow* sound. Point out that the words *snow* and *town* are in dark print.

Part B: Tell students they will write words that name pictures. Have students point to the town and say the picture name. Then, have students point to the words in dark print in the sentence above. Ask questions that help students choose and write the word *town*. Repeat with the picture of the snow.

Part C: Tell students they will write words for pictures whose names have the diphthong *ow*. Review the vowel sounds for the diphthong *ow*. Then, identify the picture of the cow. Have students repeat the word. Say the picture name again, stressing the *ow* sound: /k/-/ow/-/ow/. Have students tell whether they hear a long *o* or an *ow* sound. Next, tell students that *cow* is spelled *c, o, w*. Help them find the word in the list, write it on the line, and cross out the word once it is chosen. Continue the process with the remaining pictures by identifying the picture, the vowel sound, and the spelling of the name. When the students are done, have them circle the pictures in which the diphthong *ow* stands for the long *o* sound.

Intermediate

Part A: Follow the directions in Part A of the Beginning section.

Part B: Tell students they will write words that name pictures. Then, help students identify the pictures. Have them complete the section with a partner.

Part C: Tell students they will write words for pictures whose names have the diphthong *ow*. Review the vowel sounds for the diphthong *ow*. Then, identify the picture of the cow. Have students repeat the word. Say the picture name again, stressing the *ow* sound: /k/-/ow/-/ow/. Have students tell whether they hear a long *o* or an *ow* sound. Next, tell students that *cow* is spelled *c, o, w*. Help them find the word in the list, write it on the line, and cross out the word once it is chosen. Help students identify the names of the remaining pictures. Ask students to work with a partner to complete the page.

Advanced

Part A: Distribute page 63. Direct students to look at the first picture. Read the sentence aloud and have students repeat it. Invite students to talk about the picture. Repeat the sentence, stressing the sounds for the diphthong *ow* in each word: *The /sn/-/ō/-/ō/ fell on the /t/-/ow/-/ow/-/n/*. Remind students that *snow* has the long *o* sound and *town* has the *ow* sound. Point out that the words *snow* and *town* are in dark print.

Parts B and C: Read aloud the directions. Ask students to skim the page to see if they have a question about any of the words. Have students complete the page independently.

EXTENSION

Write *crow* and *cow* on the board. Point out the sound of *ow* in each word. Then, invite students to dictate a story about a crow and a cow. Challenge them to use as many words with the diphthong *ow* as they can.

Diphthong *ow*

A. Read the sentence.

     The **snow** fell on the **town**.

B. Write the name of each picture. Use the words in dark print above.

1.

2.

_____   _____

C. Write the word that names the picture. Then, circle the pictures whose names have the long *o* sound.

bowl   mow   clown   crown   blow   cow

3.    **4.**    **5.**

_____   _____   _____

6.    **7.**    **8.**

_____   _____   _____

Sounds of *c*

INTRODUCTION

Display a picture of a city. Say: *This is a city.* Have students repeat the sentence. Repeat with a picture of a cab. Write *city* and *cab* on the board. Underline the letter *c* in each word. Explain that the letter *c* can have two sounds. Tell students they will hear /s/ or soft *c* when *c* is before *e, i,* or *y*. They will hear /k/ or hard *c* when *c* is before any other letter.

 Invite students to describe the things they would find in a city in their native country.

Beginning

Part A: Distribute page 65. Direct students to look at the first picture. Read the sentence aloud and have students repeat it. Then, pass the picture of the city to each student and invite the student to say the sentence individually. Ask the following questions about the picture:
• *Is the cab at a farm?*
• *Is the cab in a city?*
• *Can you ride in a cab?*
• *Can you ride in a cat?*

Repeat the sentence. Remind students that *c* makes the /s/ or soft *c* sound before the letters *e, i,* or *y*, and the /k/ or hard *c* sound before any other letter. Point out that the words *cab* and *city* are in dark print.

Part B: Tell students they will write words that name pictures. Have students point to the city and say the picture name. Then, have students point to the words in dark print in the sentence above. Ask questions that help students choose and write the word *city*. Repeat with the picture of the cab.

Part C: Tell students they will sort words that have the /k/ or /s/ sound for the letter *c*. Identify the picture of the *cent*. Have students repeat the word. Say the picture name again, stressing the /s/ sound: */s/-/s/-/ent/*. Ask what letter follows *c*. Ask questions that help students write *cent* in the correct column. Continue the process with the remaining pictures by identifying the picture and the letter that follows *c*.

Intermediate

Part A: Follow the directions in Part A the Beginning section.

Part B: Tell students they will write words that name pictures. Then, help students identify the pictures. Have them complete the section with a partner.

Part C: Tell students they will sort words for pictures whose names have the /k/ or /s/ sound for the letter *c*. Have students point to each picture and word as you read them aloud. Ask students to repeat the word after you. Then, have them identify the letter that follows *c*. Ask students to work with a partner to write the words in the correct column once the words have been identified.

Advanced

Part A: Distribute page 65. Direct students to look at the first picture. Read the sentence aloud and have students repeat it. Invite students to talk about the picture. Repeat the sentence. Remind students that *c* makes the /s/ or soft *c* sound before the letters *e, i,* or *y*, and the /k/ or hard *c* sound before any other letter. Point out that the words *cab* and *city* are in dark print.

Parts B and C: Read aloud the directions. Ask students to skim the page to see if they have a question about any of the words. Have students complete the page independently.

EXTENSION

Invite students to make rubbings of the front and back of a penny using a crayon. Write *cent* and *crayon* on the board and underline the *c* in each word. Ask students which letters follow the *c* and review the rules for when *c* makes the /k/ or /s/ sounds.

Name _____   Date _____

Sounds of *c*

A. Read the sentence.

We rode in a **cab** in the **city**.

B. Write the name of each picture. Use the words in dark print above.

1.

2.

_____   _____

C. Does the word have a soft *c* or a hard *c* sound? Write the word in the correct column.

cent   cut   can   corn

fence   pencil   mice   cat

3. Words with soft *c*   **4.** Words with hard *c*

_____   _____

_____   _____

_____   _____

_____   _____

Sounds of g

NOTE: Students whose native language is Chinese, French, Greek, or Spanish may have problems with the /g/ or /j/ sounds.

INTRODUCTION

Display a picture of a garden. Say: *This is a garden.* Have students repeat the sentence. Repeat with a picture of a gerbil. Write *garden* and *gerbil* on the board. Underline the letter *g* in each word. Explain that the letter *g* can have two sounds. Tell students they will hear /j/ or soft *g* when *g* is before *e, i,* or *y.* They will hear /g/ or hard *g* when *g* is before any other letter.

 Invite students to describe the fruits and vegetables they would find in a garden in their native country.

Beginning

Part A: Distribute page 67. Direct students to look at the first picture. Read the sentence aloud and have students repeat it. Then, pass the picture of the gerbil to each student and invite the student to say the sentence individually. Ask the following questions about the picture:
• *Is the gerbil in a garden?*
• *Is the gerbil on a stage?*

Repeat the sentence. Remind students that *g* makes the /j/ or soft *g* sound before the letters *e, i,* or *y,* and the /g/ or hard *g* sound before any other letter. Point out that the words *gerbil* and *garden* are in dark print.

Part B: Tell students they will write words that name pictures. Have students point to the garden and say the picture name. Then, have students point to the words in dark print in the sentence above. Ask questions that help students choose and write the word *garden.* Repeat with the picture of the gerbil.

Part C: Tell students they will sort words that have the /g/ or /j/ sound for the letter *g.* Identify the picture of the gem. Have students repeat the word. Say the picture name again, stressing the /j/ sound: */j/-/j/-/em/.* Ask what letter follows *g.* Ask questions that help students write *gem* in the correct column. Continue the process with the remaining pictures by identifying the picture and the letter that follows *g.*

Intermediate

Part A: Follow the directions in Part A of the Beginning section.

Part B: Tell students they will write words that name pictures. Then, help students identify the pictures. Have them complete the section with a partner.

Part C: Tell students they will write words for pictures whose names have the /g/ or /j/ sound for the letter *g.* Have students point to each picture and word as you read them aloud. Ask students to repeat the word after you. Then, have them identify the letter that follows *g.* Ask students to work with a partner to write the words in the correct column once the words have been identified.

Advanced

Part A: Distribute page 67. Direct students to look at the first picture. Read the sentence aloud and have students repeat it. Invite students to talk about the picture. Repeat the sentence. Remind students that *g* makes the /j/ or soft *g* sound before the letters *e, i,* or *y,* and the /g/ or hard *g* sound before any other letter. Point out that the words *gerbil* and *garden* are in dark print.

Parts B and C: Read aloud the directions. Ask students to skim the page to see if they have a question about any of the words. Have students complete the page independently.

EXTENSION

Challenge students to solve riddles. Give clues about one of the pictures on page 67 for students to solve. The student who solves it then tells a new riddle.

Sounds of *g*

A. Read the sentence.

The **gerbil** is in the **garden**.

B. Write the name of each picture. Use the words in dark print above.

1.
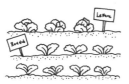

_____

2.

_____

C. Does the word have a soft *g* or a hard *g* sound? Write the word in the correct column.

gem

giant

gum

gas

dog

cage

stage

wig

3. Words with soft *g*

_____

_____

_____

_____

4. Words with hard *g*

_____

_____

_____

_____

Sounds of *s*

NOTE: Students whose native language is Chinese, French, Greek, Japanese, Korean, Spanish, Urdu, or Vietnamese may have problems with /s/, /z/, or /sh/ sounds.

INTRODUCTION
Display the following items: soap, sugar, cheese, tissues. Identify each and have students repeat the name. Then, write the name of each item on the board. Underline the letters *s* or *ss* in each word. Explain that the letter *s* can also have the /z/ sound in *nose* and the /sh/ sound in *tissue*.

 Invite students to say *sugar* in their native language.

Beginning
Part A: Distribute page 69. Direct students to look at the picture of the girl with the soap, sugar, and cheese. Read the sentence aloud and have students repeat it. Then, pass the soap to each student and invite the student to say the sentence individually. Ask the following questions about the picture:
• *Did Kiko buy cheese? Point to it.*
• *Did Kiko buy soap? Point to it.*
• *Did Kiko buy tissues?*
• *Did Kiko buy sugar? Point to it.*

Repeat the sentence. Remind students that *s* makes the /s/, /z/, and /sh/ sounds. Point out that the words *soap, sugar,* and *cheese* are in dark print.

Part B: Tell students they will write words that name pictures. Have students point to the sugar and say the picture name. Then, have students point to the words in dark print in the sentence above. Ask questions that help students choose and write the word *sugar*. Repeat with the pictures of the soap and cheese.

Part C: Tell students they will write *s, z,* or *sh* to show the sound for *s* in words. Identify the picture of the seal. Have students repeat the word. Say the picture name again, stressing the /s/ sound: /s/-/s/-/ēl/. Have them write *s* on the line. Continue the process with the remaining pictures by identifying the picture and the sound for *s*.

Intermediate
Part A: Follow the directions in Part A of the Beginning section.

Part B: Tell students they will write words that name pictures. Then, help students identify the pictures. Have them complete the section with a partner.

Part C: Tell students they will write *s, z,* or *sh* to show the sound for *s* in words. Have students point to the picture of the seal. Ask students to repeat the word after you. Say the picture name again, stressing the /s/ sound: /s/-/s/-/ēl/. Have them write *s* on the line. Help students identify the names of the remaining pictures. Ask students to work with a partner to complete the page.

Advanced
Part A: Distribute page 69. Direct students to look at the picture of the girl with the soap, sugar, and cheese. Read the sentence aloud and have students repeat it. Invite students to talk about the picture. Repeat the sentence. Remind students that s makes the /s/, /z/, and /sh/ sounds. Point out that the words *soap, sugar,* and *cheese* are in dark print.

Parts B and C: Read aloud the directions. Ask students to skim the page to see if they have a question about any of the words. Have students complete the page independently.

EXTENSION
Duplicate additional copies of the page and cut out the pictures. Invite students to play Concentration. Challenge them to match pictures whose names have the same sound of *s*.

Sounds of *s*

A. Read the sentence.

   Kiko bought  **soap**,   **sugar**, and  **cheese**.

B. Write the name of each picture. Use the words in dark print above.

1.

2.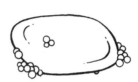

3.

_____   _____   _____

C. Write *s*, *z*, or *sh* on the line to tell the sound that *s* makes in each picture name.

4.

5.

6.

7.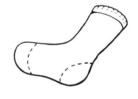

seal   hose   mission   sock

_____   _____   _____   _____

8.

9.

10.

11.

music   tissue   sun   rose

_____   _____   _____   _____

Digraphs *ch* and *wh*

NOTE: Students whose native language is Chinese, French, Greek, Japanese, or Spanish may have problems with *ch* and *wh* words.

INTRODUCTION

Invite students to play telephone. Tell them you will say one word that they are to share with others one at a time. Then, whisper *children* in one student's ear and have the person pass the message to another student. After the last student has shared the word, point out that students were whispering. Write *whisper* and *children* on the board and underline *wh* and *ch*. Explain that some letters work together to make new sounds. Tell students that the letters *wh* have the /wh/ sound in *whisper*, and the letters *ch* have the /ch/ sound in *children*.

 Invite students to play telephone again by whispering the word *children* in their native language.

Beginning

Part A: Distribute page 71. Direct students to look at the first picture. Read the sentence aloud and have students repeat it. Then, invite each student to whisper the sentence. Ask the following questions about the picture:
• *What are the children doing? Show me.*
• *Who is whispering? Point to them.*
• *Are the children yelling?*
• *Are the children whispering?*

Repeat the sentence, stressing the /ch/ and /wh/ sounds. Remind students that the letters *ch* make the /ch/ sound and the letters *wh* make the /wh/ sound. Point out that the words *children* and *whisper* are in dark print.

Part B: Tell students they will write words that name pictures. Have students point to the children and say the picture name. Then, have students point to the words in dark print in the sentence above. Ask questions that help students choose and write the word *children*. Repeat with the picture that shows a whisper.

Part C: Tell students they will choose words whose names begin with *ch* or *wh* to complete sentences. Read aloud the first sentence with the rebus. Say

whistle, stressing the /wh/ sound: /wh/-/wh/-/is/-/uhl/. Say *whistle* again for them to repeat. Tell students that *whistle* is spelled *w, h, i, s, t, l, e*. Help them find the word in the list, write it on the line, and cross out the word once it is chosen. Continue the process with the remaining sentences.

Intermediate

Part A: Follow the directions in Part A of the Beginning section, but substitute these questions:
• *What are the students doing?*
• *Who is whispering?*

Part B: Tell students they will write words that name pictures. Then, help students identify the pictures. Have them complete the section with a partner.

Part C: Tell students they will choose words whose names begin with *ch* or *wh* to complete sentences. Say the word *whistle*, stressing the /wh/ sound: /wh/-/wh/-/is/-/uhl/. Say the word again and have students repeat the word as they point to it. Then, repeat the process with the other words. Explain that all the words in the box begin with *ch* or *wh*. Next, read aloud the first sentence with the rebus. Pause to allow students time to write their answer. Continue the process with the remaining sentences.

Advanced

Part A: Distribute page 71. Direct students to look at the first picture. Read the sentence aloud and have students repeat it. Invite students to talk about the picture. Repeat the sentence, stressing the /ch/ and /wh/ sounds. Remind students that the letters *ch* make the /ch/ sound and the letters *wh* make the /wh/ sound. Point out that the words *children* and *whisper* are in dark print.

Parts B and C: Read aloud the directions. Ask students to skim the page to see if they have a question about any of the words. Have students complete the page independently.

EXTENSION

Invite students to play telephone again. Challenge them to send messages in which a sentence has both a word that begins with *ch* and with *wh*.

Digraphs *ch* and *wh*

A. Read the sentence.

The **children** **whisper** quietly.

B. Write the name of each picture. Use the words in dark print above.

1.

_____

2.

_____

C. Write a word from the box to complete each sentence.

chick   whistle   chair

3. The children blow a _____.

4. The children sit on a _____.

5. The children hold a baby _____.

Digraphs *sh* and *th*

NOTE: Students whose native language is Chinese, French, Italian, Japanese, Korean, Urdu, or Vietnamese may have problems with *sh* and *th* words.

INTRODUCTION

Invite a student wearing a brightly colored shirt to stand. Say: *I think that shirt is [color].* Have students repeat the sentence. Write *shirt* on the board and underline *sh.* Explain that the letters *sh* have the /sh/ sound in *shirt.* Next, write *think* and *that* on the board. Underline the *th* in each word. Point out that *th* can have two sounds. Tell students it can have the whispered /th/ in *think* and the voiced /th/ in *that.* Repeat each word several times for students to listen to the initial sounds.

 Invite students to name the clothes they are wearing in their native language.

 Some students have difficulty hearing the difference between the sounds of *sh* and *th*, *sh* and *s*, *sh* and *ch*, *th* and *z*, *th* and *t*, and *th* and *s*.

Beginning

Part A: Distribute page 73. Direct students to look at the first picture. Read the sentence aloud and have students repeat it. Then, invite each student to repeat the sentence. Ask the following questions about the picture:
• *What is the girl looking at? Point to it.*
• *How much does the shirt cost? Point to it.*
• *Is the girl looking at that shirt?*
• *Is that shirt thirteen dollars?*

Repeat the sentence, stressing the /th/ and /sh/ sounds. Remind students that the letters *th* make the beginning sounds in *that* and *thirteen*, and the letters *sh* make the beginning sound in *shirt.* Point out that the words *that, shirt,* and *thirteen* are in dark print.

Part B: Tell students they will write words that name pictures. Have students point to the shirt and say the picture name. Then, have students point to the words in dark print in the sentence above. Ask questions that help students choose and write the word *shirt.* Repeat with the pictures that show *that* and *thirteen.*

Part C: Tell students that they will circle sentences that tell about pictures. Explain that the pictures show something that begins with *sh* or *th.* Then, have students look at the first picture. Read aloud the sentences, pausing to let students repeat each one. Ask questions that help students choose and circle the correct sentence. Continue the process with the remaining pictures and sentences.

Intermediate

Part A: Follow the directions in Part A of the Beginning section, but substitute these questions:
• *What is the girl looking at?*
• *How much does that shirt cost?*

Part B: Tell students they will write words that name pictures. Then, help students identify the pictures. Have them complete the section with a partner.

Part C: Tell students that they will circle sentences that tell about pictures. Explain that the pictures show something that begins with *sh* or *th.* Then, have students look at the first picture. Read aloud the sentences, omitting the word that identifies the correct sentence. Challenge students to silently read those words and circle their answer. Continue the process with the remaining pictures and sentences.

Advanced

Part A: Distribute page 73. Direct students to look at the first picture. Read the sentence aloud and have students repeat it. Invite students to talk about the picture. Repeat the sentence, stressing the /sh/ and /th/ sounds. Remind students that the letters *th* make the beginning sounds in *that* and *thirteen*, and the letters *sh* make the beginning sound in *shirt.* Point out that the words *that, shirt,* and *thirteen* are in dark print.

Parts B and C: Read aloud the directions. Ask students to skim the page to see if they have a question about any of the words. Have students complete the page independently.

EXTENSION

Write the words *this, that, these,* and *those* on cards. Explain that many words that begin with the digraph *th* tell where things are. Pass out the cards to students. Have them use the words to tell the relative location of items in the classroom. (*I like this book.*)

Digraphs *sh* and *th*

A. Read the sentence.

That **shirt** is **thirteen** dollars.

B. Write the name of each picture. Use the words in dark print above.

1.

2.

3.

_____   _____   _____

C. Read each sentence. Circle the sentence that matches the picture.

4. Look at those chicks.

Look at those ships.

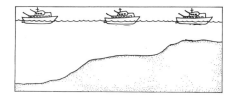

5. A shell is on the sand.

A sheep is on the sand.

6. The rose has a thorn.

The rose has a thumb.

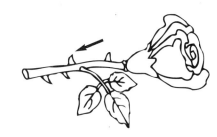

Nouns

INTRODUCTION

Write the column headings *Person, Place,* and *Thing* on the board. Invite students to name people that are in the school, such as a teacher, nurse, or principal. Write each name on the board as it is identified. Guide students to complete the chart by naming places and things students find at school. Tell students that the words on the board are nouns. Explain that nouns name a person, place, or thing.

 Invite students to compare specific places in the United States, such as stores, with those in their native country.

Beginning

Part A: Distribute page 75. Direct students to look at the first picture. Read the sentence aloud and have students repeat it. Ask the following questions about the picture:
- *Who is at the farm? Point to it.*
- *What is the boy feeding? Point to it.*
- *Is the goat at the farm or at the park?*

Tell students that *boy, goat,* and *farm* are nouns. Write them in the appropriate columns on the board. Remind students that nouns name a person, place, or thing.

Part B: Tell students they will write the words in dark print on lines to tell if they name a person, place, or thing. Have students point to the word *boy* and repeat it. Ask questions that help students decide if the word names a person, place, or thing. Guide them to write it in on the correct line. Repeat with the remaining words.

Part C: Tell students they will sort words to tell if they name a person, place or thing. Identify the picture of the peach and have students repeat the word. Ask questions that help students realize that *peach* names a thing. Guide them to write *peach* in the *Thing* column. Continue the process with the remaining pictures and words.

Intermediate

Part A: Follow the directions in Part A of the Beginning section, but substitute these questions:
- *Who is at the farm?*
- *What is the boy feeding?*
- *Where does a goat live?*

Part B: Tell students they will write the words in dark print on lines to tell if they name a person, place, or thing. Have students point to the word *boy* and repeat it. Ask questions that help students decide if the word names a person, place, or thing. Guide them to write it in on the correct line. Review the remaining words in dark print and have students complete the section.

Part C: Tell students they will sort words to tell if they name a person, place, or thing. Identify the picture of the peach and have students repeat the word. Ask questions that help students realize that *peach* names a thing. Guide them to write *peach* in the *Thing* column. Identify the remaining pictures and pause to allow students to write their answers.

Advanced

Part A: Distribute page 75. Direct students to look at the first picture. Read the sentence aloud and have students repeat it. Invite students to talk about the picture. Tell students that *boy, goat,* and *farm* are nouns. Remind students that nouns are words that name a person, place, or thing.

Parts B and C: Read aloud the directions. Ask students to skim the page to see if they have a question about any of the words. Have students complete the page independently.

EXTENSION

Refer to the list of nouns compiled on the board. Challenge each student to say a sentence that names a person, place, and thing.

Language Arts

Nouns

A. Read the sentence.

 The **boy** feeds a **goat** at the **farm**.

B. Read each word in dark print. Does the word name a person, a place, or a thing? Write it on the line.

1. person   **2.** place   **3.** thing

_____   _____   _____

C. Does the picture show a person, place, or thing? Write the word in the correct column.

peach

kitchen

truck

girl

vet

zoo

book

park

4. Person   **5.** Place   **6.** Thing

_____   _____   _____

_____   _____   _____

_____   _____   _____

Proper Nouns

INTRODUCTION

Invite a volunteer to stand. Say: *(Name) is a (girl/boy)*. Write the student's name and gender on the board. Explain to students that some words name a special person, place, or thing and that these nouns begin with capital letters. Explain that the name on the board is a special noun, or proper noun, and the word *boy/girl* is a plain noun. Guide students to understand the difference because of the capital letter. Repeat the process using these sentences: *The name of our school is (school name). The school is on (street name).* Point out that some names, like streets and buildings, have two words that must be capitalized.

Beginning

Part A: Distribute page 77. Direct students to look at the first picture. Read the sentence aloud and have students repeat it. Ask the following questions about the picture:
• *Is the name of the boy Marco?*
• *Does Marco live on South Street?*

Tell students that *Marco* and *South Street* are proper nouns that begin with capital letters. Remind them that some names, like streets and buildings, have two words that must be capitalized. Remind students that nouns are words that name a person, place, or thing.

Part B: Tell students they will write the proper nouns in dark print on lines to tell what kind of noun they are. Have students point to and say the word *boy*. Guide them to find the word in dark print that names a boy and write it on the line. Repeat with the word *street*.

Part C: Tell students they will circle proper nouns in sentences that are not written correctly. Then, they will rewrite them with capital letters. Read aloud the first sentence. Have students repeat it. Help them realize that *Marco* is the special name of a person and have them circle it. Then, have them write it correctly on the line. Continue the process with the remaining sentences.

Intermediate

Part A: Follow the directions in Part A of the Beginning section, but substitute these questions:
• *What is the name of the boy?*
• *On what street does the boy live?*

Part B: Tell students they will write the special names in dark print on lines to tell what kind of noun they are. Have students point to and say the nouns. Review the words in dark print and have students complete the section independently.

Part C: Tell students they will circle proper nouns in sentences that are not written correctly. Then, they will rewrite them with capital letters. Read aloud the first sentence. Have students repeat it. Help them realize that *Marco* is the special name of a person and have them circle it and write it correctly. Read the remaining sentences and pause to allow students time to circle and write their answers.

Advanced

Part A: Distribute page 77. Direct students to look at the first picture. Read the sentence aloud and have students repeat it. Invite students to talk about the picture. Ask students how they know that *Marco* and *South Street* are proper nouns. Remind them that some names, like streets and buildings, have two words that must be capitalized. Remind students that nouns are words that name a person, place, or thing.

Parts B and C: Read aloud the directions. Ask students to skim the page to see if they have a question about any of the words. Have students complete the page independently.

EXTENSION

Have students draw a picture of an adult in their family. Help them brainstorm names that each person is called. For example, a mother might have several names: *Mother, Mrs. Ruiz, Aunt Lydia, Lydia,* etc.

Proper Nouns

A. Read the sentence.

Marco lives on **South** **Street**.

B. Read each word in dark print. What kind of noun is it? Write it on the line.

1. boy

_____

2. street

_____

C. Circle the names that should be written with capital letters. Then, write the names with capital letters.

3. marco takes his dog to the vet.

_____

4. The name of the vet is dr. smith.

_____

5. marco walks on cook road.

_____

6. He walks by oak library.

_____

7. He waves to mrs. kim.

_____

Plurals

INTRODUCTION

Display a box of crayons. Hold up one crayon and say: *I have one crayon.* Have students repeat the sentence. Then, hold up two crayons. Say: *I have two crayons.* Write *crayon* and *crayons* on the board. Say each word and show the corresponding number of crayons. Underline the *s* in *crayons* and explain that *crayon* is a noun; it names a thing. Tell students that words that mean more than one usually end in *s.* Reinforce the skill by saying one of the words and having volunteers hold up the corresponding number of crayons as they repeat the word. Repeat with empty boxes to introduce that *es* is added to words ending in *s, x, ss, ch,* or *sh.* Next, explain that *es* is also added to words ending in *y,* but the *y* is first changed to *i.*

Beginning

Part A: Distribute page 79. Direct students to look at the first picture. Read the sentence aloud and have students repeat it. Ask the following questions about the picture:
• *How many logs do you see? Hold up the number of fingers to show me.*
• *How many frogs do you see? Hold up the number of fingers to show me.*

Have students circle the words *frogs* and *log.* Point out that both words are nouns. Explain to students that *frogs* means more than one frog because it ends in *s.* Point out that *log* means only one.

Part B: Tell students they will write the words in dark print on lines to show which word names one and which word names more than one. Read the word *log.* Have students point to it and repeat it. Ask questions that help students realize that since there is no *s* on *log,* it is not a plural noun. Guide them to write it on the line labeled *one.* Read the word *frogs.* Have students point to it and repeat it. Ask questions that help students realize that since there is an *s* on *frogs,* it is a plural noun. Guide them to write it on the line labeled *more than one.*

Part C: Tell students they will choose and circle words to complete sentences. Explain that there are two words in the parentheses they will choose from—one word names one and the other names more than one. Read aloud the first sentence without the answer choices. Ask questions that help students use context clues to choose the answer. Guide students to circle *ducks.* Continue the process with the remaining sentences.

Intermediate

Part A: Follow the directions in Part A of the Beginning section, but substitute these questions:
• *Do you see one or two frogs?*
• *Do you see one or two logs?*

Part B: Tell students they will write the words in dark print on lines to show which word names one and which word names more than one. Read the words *frogs* and *log.* Have students point to the words and repeat them. Ask questions that help students realize that because *frogs* ends in *s,* it is a plural noun. Have students complete the section.

Part C: Tell students they will choose and circle words to complete sentences. Explain that there are two words in the parentheses they will choose from—one word names one and the other names more than one. Read aloud the first sentence without the answer choices. Ask questions that help students use context clues to choose the answer. Guide students to circle *ducks.* Read the remaining sentences with the answer choices and pause to allow students time to circle their answers.

Advanced

Part A: Distribute page 79. Direct students to look at the first picture. Read the sentence aloud and have students repeat it. Invite students to talk about the picture. Tell students that *frogs* and *log* are nouns. Explain to students that *frogs* means more than one frog because it ends in *s.* Point out that *log* means only one. Briefly review the rules for adding *s* or *es.*

Parts B and C: Read aloud the directions. Ask students to skim the page to see if they have a question about any of the words. Briefly review the rules for adding *s* or *es.* Have students complete the page independently.

EXTENSION

Write these words on the board: *bench, box, brush, fox, baby,* and *paint.* Challenge students to write the plural form of each word. Then, ask pairs of students to use the words in a short story. Invite them to draw a picture to go along with their story.

Name _____ Date _____

Plurals

A. Read the sentence.

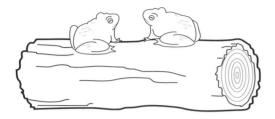

The **frogs** sit on a **log**.

B. Read each word in dark print. Does the word name one or more than one? Write the word on the line.

1. one

_____

2. more than one

_____

C. Circle the word that completes the sentence correctly.

3. Some (duck, ducks) swim past.

4. They flap their (wing, wings).

5. They try to catch some (fly, flies) to eat.

6. The noise scares one (frog, frogs).

7. It jumps into the (lake, lakes).

Present Tense Verbs

INTRODUCTION

Invite a student to draw a picture on the board. As the student draws, write *(Name) draws on the board.* Invite a second student to draw on the board. Write *(Name) and (Name) draw on the board.* Circle the verb in each sentence. Tell students that verbs are words that show action. Pantomime other actions for students to name. Then, guide students to understand that when the action happens now, or in the present, a verb paired with a singular noun ends in *s*, while a verb paired with a plural noun or two nouns has no special ending. Review the sentences on the board to further explain the concept of verb endings in the present tense.

 Invite students to say an action word in their native language and to act it out. Have the others guess the movement.

Beginning

Part A: Distribute page 81. Direct students to look at the first picture. Read the sentences aloud and have students repeat them. Ask the following questions about the pictures and sentences:
• *Which picture shows one dog? Point to it.*
• *Look at the word in dark print under that picture. Does it end in* s?
• *Which picture shows two dogs? Point to it.*
• *Look at the word in dark print under that picture. Does it end in* s?

Remind students that *runs* and *run* are action words, or verbs. Review that when the action is happening now, a verb paired with a singular noun ends in *s*, while a verb paired with a plural noun has no special ending.

Part B: Remind students that the words in dark print are action words, or verbs, and describe an action that is happening now. Tell students they will write the words in dark print on lines to show which word would be paired with a noun that names one and which would be paired with a noun that names more than one. Read the word *runs*. Have students point to it and repeat it. Ask questions that help students realize that since there is an *s* on *runs*, it is paired with a singular noun. Guide them to write it on the line labeled *one*. Repeat with *run*.

Part C: Tell students they will choose and circle words to complete sentences. Explain that there are two verbs in the parentheses they will choose from—one would be used with a singular noun and the other with a plural noun. Read aloud the first sentence. Ask questions that help students examine the nouns to choose the answer. Guide students to circle *walk*. Continue the process with the remaining sentences.

Intermediate

Part A: Follow the directions in Part A of the Beginning section.

Part B: Follow the directions in Part B of the Beginning section.

Part C: Tell students they will choose and circle words to complete sentences. Explain that there are two verbs in the parentheses they will choose from—one would be used with a singular noun and the other with a plural noun. Read aloud the first sentence. Ask questions that help students examine the nouns to choose the answer. Guide students to circle *walk*. Read aloud the remaining sentences with the answer choices and pause to allow students time to write their answers.

Advanced

Part A: Distribute page 81. Direct students to look at the first picture. Read the sentences aloud and have students repeat them. Invite students to talk about the pictures. Remind students that *runs* and *run* are actions words, or verbs. Review that when the action is happening now, a verb paired with a singular noun ends in *s*, while a verb paired with a plural noun has no special ending.

Parts B and C: Read aloud the directions. Ask students to skim the page to see if they have a question about any of the words. Have students complete the page independently.

EXTENSION

Direct students to reread the sentences about the dogs. Then, write the following sentence on the board: *I run in the park.* Explain that when a present tense verb is paired with *I* or *you*, the verb does not end in *s*.

Present Tense Verbs

A. Read the sentences.

The dog **runs**.   The dogs **run**.

B. Read each word in dark print. Which word is used with one? Which word is used with more than one? Write the word on the line.

1. one   **2.** more than one

_____   _____

C. Circle the word that completes the sentence correctly.

3. Chau and her dad (walk, walks) in the woods.

4. They (eat, eats) lunch.

5. Chau (see, sees) a raccoon.

6. The raccoon (sleep, sleeps).

7. Chau and her dad (laugh, laughs).

Past Tense Verbs

INTRODUCTION

Ask students if they talked on the phone yesterday. Invite volunteers to tell whom they talked with: *I talked with (name).* Write *talked* on the board. Explain that *ed* is added to the end of most words to show an action that happened in the past. Challenge students to name other actions they did yesterday and write the words ending in *ed* on the board.

 Invite students to say a past-tense action in their native language and pantomime the action for others to guess.

Beginning

Part A: Distribute page 83. Direct students to look at the first picture. Read the sentence aloud and have students repeat it. Ask the following questions about the picture:
• *What did Ben do yesterday? Show me.*
• *Does the picture show that Ben talked?*
• *Does the picture show that Ben skated?*

Tell students that *skated* is an action word. Remind them that the *ed* ending is a clue that the action happened in the past.

Part B: Tell students they will write words to show actions that happened in the past. Have students point to the word *climb*. Read it out loud and have students repeat it. Then, tell students they need to rewrite the word to show the action happened yesterday. Ask questions that help students rewrite the word and add *ed*. Repeat with the word *pull*.

Part C: Tell students they will choose and circle words that show past actions to complete sentences. Explain that there are two verbs in the parentheses they will choose from—one shows action in the present and one shows action in the past. Read aloud the first sentence with the answer choices. Ask questions that help students recognize that the *ed* ending is a clue. Guide students to circle *visited*. Continue the process with the remaining sentences.

Intermediate

Part A: Follow the directions in Part A of the Beginning section, but substitute this question:
• *What did Ben do yesterday?*

Part B: Tell students they will write words to show actions that happened in the past. Have students identify the actions. Then, have students point to and read the words. Ask questions that help students rewrite the word and add *ed*. Have them write the last word independently.

Part C: Tell students they will circle words that show past actions to complete sentences. Explain that there are two verbs in the parentheses they will choose from—one shows action in the present and one shows action in the past. Read aloud the first sentence with the answer choices. Ask questions that help students recognize that the *ed* ending is a clue. Guide students to circle *visited*. Read aloud the remaining sentences, and pause to allow students time to circle their answers.

Advanced

Part A: Distribute page 83. Direct students to look at the first picture. Read the sentence aloud and have students repeat it. Invite students to talk about the picture. Tell students that *skated* is an action word. Remind them that the *ed* ending is a clue that the action happened in the past.

Parts B and C: Read aloud the directions. Ask students to skim the page to see if they have a question about any of the words. Have students complete the page independently.

EXTENSION

Pair students and have them tell about activities they participated in yesterday.

Past Tense Verbs

A. Read the sentence.

Ben **skated** yesterday.

B. Write the words to show that it happened in the past.

1.

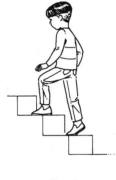

climb

_____

2.

pull

_____

C. Make each sentence tell about the past. Circle the correct word.

3. Ben (visits, visited) a friend yesterday.

4. They (played, plays) games.

5. Ben (walks, walked) home later.

6. He (talked, talks) with his father.

7. Then, Ben (works, worked) on homework.

Pronouns

INTRODUCTION

Invite students to draw a picture of their favorite food. As volunteers display their drawings, use the sentence frame: *(Name) likes to eat (food).* Repeat the sentence using a pronoun in place of the name. Ask questions that guide students to understand how the sentence changed. Point out that pronouns can take the place of nouns. Write the subject pronouns on the board *(I, you, he, she, it, we, they).* Give examples of each in a sentence.

Beginning

Part A: Distribute page 85. Direct students to look at the picture of the two girls reading. Read the sentences aloud and have students repeat them. Ask the following questions about the sentences:
• *Where are the names of the girls? Point to them.*
• *Look at the second sentence. What word is in dark print? Point to it.*
• *Does the word* they *take the place of the names* Lana and Pam*?*

Tell students that *they* is a pronoun that takes the place of the names *Lana and Pam.* Remind them of the other pronouns on the board.

Part B: Tell students they will circle pronouns that name the people in pictures. Direct students to look at the picture of the girl. Ask questions that help students choose the correct pronoun. Repeat with the next picture.

Part C: Tell students they will write pronouns that take the place of nouns. Read the words in the box. Then read aloud the first sentence. Ask students to repeat the underlined word or words. Ask questions about the phrase to help students choose the correct pronoun. Help them find the word in the list, write it on the line, and cross out the word once it is chosen. Continue the process with the remaining sentences.

Intermediate

Part A: Follow the directions in Part A of the Beginning section, but substitute these questions:
• *What are the names of the girls?*
• *Which word is in dark print in the second sentence?*
• *Which word can take the place of the names of the girls?*

Part B: Follow the directions in Part B of the Beginning section.

Part C: Tell students they will write pronouns that take the place of nouns. Read the words in the box. Then, read aloud the first sentence. Ask students to repeat the underlined word. Ask questions about the word to help students choose the correct pronoun. Read aloud the remaining sentences and pause to allow students time to write their answers.

Advanced

Part A: Distribute page 85. Direct students to look at the picture of the two girls reading. Read the sentences aloud and have students repeat them. Invite students to talk about the picture. Tell students that *they* is a pronoun that takes the place of the names *Lana and Pam.* Remind them of the other pronouns on the board.

Parts B and C: Read aloud the directions. Ask students to skim the page to see if they have a question about any of the words. Have students complete the page independently.

EXTENSION

Say sentences about the students using their names. Challenge the students to repeat the sentences using pronouns. *(Rita wears a red shirt. Maria and Pablo have brown eyes.)*

Pronouns

A. Read the sentences.

Lana and Pam read a book.

They read a book.

B. Circle the word that matches the pictures.

1.

she   we

2.

they   I

C. Write a word from the box that can take the place of the underlined word or words.

They	She	He	It

3. <u>Lana</u> got the book from school. _____

4. <u>The book</u> is about animals. _____

5. <u>Jay</u> wants to read the book, too. _____

6. <u>Lana and Pam</u> will read the book first. _____

Adjectives That Compare

INTRODUCTION

Invite students to draw a circle on paper. Invite one student to show the circle. Say: *This circle is small.* Tell students that *small* describes how the circle looks. Continue to explain that a word that describes a noun is called an adjective. Next, invite a second student to hold up his or her circle and say a sentence using *smaller* to compare the two. Have a third student join the group. Say a sentence to indicate the smallest circle. Write *small, smaller,* and *smallest* on the board. Explain that *er* is added to words to compare two persons or things, and *est* is added to compare more than two persons or things.

Beginning

Part A: Distribute page 87. Direct students to look at the pictures of the dogs. Read the sentences aloud and have students repeat them. Ask the following questions about the sentences and pictures:
• *Point to the word* bigger. *Is this dog bigger than the white dog?*
• *Point to the word* biggest. *Is this dog the biggest dog of all the dogs you see?*

Remind students that adjectives describe nouns. Tell students that *big, bigger,* and *biggest* describe the sizes of the dogs. Point out that *er* is added to words to compare two persons or things, and *est* is added to compare more than two persons or things. Briefly explain that when a word ends in one vowel followed by one consonant, the consonant is doubled before *er* or *est* is added.

Part B: Tell students they will write words that describe pictures. Have students look at all three kite pictures and compare the sizes. Then, have them point to the fluffy dog. Remind them that this is the biggest dog. Then, have students point to the words in dark print in the sentences. Ask questions that help students choose and write the word *biggest* for the first kite. Repeat with the remaining pictures.

Part C: Tell students they will complete sentences by writing words that compare animals. Read aloud the first sentence without the adjective. Then, direct students to look at the word in parentheses. Ask questions that help students identify and write the correct comparative adjective. Next, tell students how to spell the word. Read the sentence with the adjective in place.

Continue the process with the remaining sentences.

Intermediate

Part A: Follow the directions in Part A of the Beginning section, but substitute these questions:
• *Is the white dog or the dog with spots bigger?*
• *Is the dog with spots or the fluffy dog bigger?*
• *Which is the biggest dog of all?*

Part B: Tell students they will write words that describe pictures. Have students look at all three kite pictures and compare the sizes. Then, have them point to the fluffy dog. Remind them that this is the biggest dog. Then, have students point to the words in dark print in the sentences. Ask questions that help students choose and write the word *biggest* for the first kite. Have students work with a partner to complete the section.

Part C: Tell students they will complete sentences by writing words that compare animals. Read aloud the first sentence without the adjective. Then, direct students to look at the word in parentheses. Ask questions that help students identify and write the correct comparative adjective. Read the sentence with the adjective in place. Read aloud the remaining sentences and pause to allow students time to write their answers.

Advanced

Part A: Distribute page 87. Direct students to look at the pictures of the dogs. Read the sentences aloud and have students repeat them. Invite students to talk about the pictures. Remind students that adjectives describe nouns. Tell students that *big, bigger,* and *biggest* describe the sizes of the dogs. Remind them that that *er* is added to words to compare two persons or things, and *est* is added to compare more than two persons or things. Briefly explain that when a word ends in one vowel followed by one consonant, the consonant is doubled before *er* or *est* is added.

Parts B and C: Read aloud the directions. Ask students to skim the page to see if they have a question about any of the words. Have students complete the page independently.

EXTENSION

Assign three students to groups. Challenge them to choose and illustrate, either through drawing or pantomiming, a comparative adjective.

Adjectives That Compare

A. Read the sentences.

   This white dog is **big**.

   This dog is **bigger** than the white dog.

   This fluffy dog is the **biggest** of all.

B. Write the word that describes each picture. Use the words in dark print above.

1.    2.   3.

_____   _____   _____

C. Complete each sentence with the correct form of the word in ( ).

4. The turtle is the _____ animal of all. (slow)

5. The cow is _____ than the goat. (big)

6. The giraffe is the _____ animal in the world. (tall)

8. A sheep has _____ wool. (soft)

Compound Words

INTRODUCTION

Display a raincoat. Lead students in a discussion of when the coat is used. Write *raincoat* on the board. Say the word and have students repeat it. Explain that *raincoat* is a compound word and that compound words are made up of two smaller words joined together. Then, write the following under the word: *rain + coat = raincoat*.

Beginning

Part A: Distribute page 89. Direct students to look at the first picture. Read the sentence aloud and have students repeat it. Ask the following questions about the picture:
• *Does the boy have a ball?*
• *Is the boy kicking the ball with his foot?*

Have students point to the word *football*. Explain that *football* is made of the two smaller words *foot* and *ball*. Remind students that a compound word is made of two smaller words joined together.

Part B: Tell students they will write the two smaller words in *football*. Direct students to look at the picture of the foot. Ask questions that help students write *foot*. Repeat with the picture of the ball.

Part C: Tell students they will write compound words. Have students point to the picture of the rainbow. Ask questions that help students identify the rainbow. Then, slowly read the words beside the picture as students point to them and repeat them. Guide students to write *rainbow* on the line. Have them say the word. Continue the process with the remaining pictures and words.

Intermediate

Part A: Follow the directions in Part A of the Beginning section, but substitute these questions:
• *What is the boy kicking?*
• *Is the boy kicking with his foot or his hand?*

Part B: Follow the directions in Part B of the Beginning section.

Part C: Have students point to the picture of the rainbow. Ask questions that help students identify the rainbow. Then, slowly read the words beside the picture as students point to them and repeat them. Guide students to write *rainbow* on the line. Have them say the word. Ask questions about the remaining pictures and pause to allow students time to write their answers. Have them say the compound words.

Advanced

Part A: Distribute page 89. Direct students to look at the first picture. Read the sentence aloud and have students repeat it. Invite students to talk about the picture. Then, have them point to the word *football*. Explain that *football* is made of the two smaller words *foot* and *ball*. Remind students that a compound word is made of two smaller words joined together.

Parts B and C: Read aloud the directions. Ask students to skim the page to see if they have a question about any of the words. Have students complete the page independently.

EXTENSION

Write a list of compound words on the board. Have students choose one to illustrate in an equation-like sentence.

Name _____   Date _____

Compound Words

A. Read the sentence.

Luke plays **football**.

B. Write the two words in **football**.

1.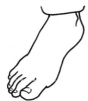

2.

_____   _____

C. Write the words together to make each compound word.

   **3.** rain + bow = _____

   **4.** sail + boat = _____

   **5.** lunch + room = _____

   **6.** birth + day = _____

Contractions

INTRODUCTION

Invite a student to put on an oversized piece of clothing. Say: *The (shirt) does not fit.* Then, write *does not* on the board. Tell students that some words in the English language can be made shorter. Erase the *o* and add the apostrophe to make the contraction *doesn't*. Read aloud the word and ask students to repeat it. Explain that the little mark that takes the place of the letter is an apostrophe. Repeat the initial sentence using the contraction *doesn't*.

Beginning

Part A: Distribute page 91. Direct students to look at the picture of the boy and girl. Read the sentences aloud and have students repeat them. Ask the following questions about the sentences:
- *Look at the first sentence. Where are the words* could not*? Point to them.*
- *Look at the second sentence. What word is in dark print? Point to it.*
- *Does the word* couldn't *take the place of the words* could not*?*
- *Is the letter* o *missing in* couldn't*?*

Tell students that *couldn't* is a contraction that is a short form for the words *could not*. Remind them that the apostrophe, the little mark in the word, shows that a letter or letters are missing.

Part B: Tell students they will draw lines to match pairs of words with their contractions. Read each pair of words and ask questions that help students find and draw lines to the corresponding contraction.

Part C: Tell students they will write contractions that make pairs of words shorter. Read the words in the box. Then, read aloud the first sentence. Ask students to repeat the underlined words. Ask questions about the phrase to help students choose the correct contraction. Have them say the word and write it on the line. Continue the process with the remaining sentences.

Intermediate

Part A: Follow the directions in Part A of the Beginning section, but substitute these questions:
- *Look at the words in dark print in the first sentence. Are the words* does not *or* could not*?*
- *Look at the word in dark print in the second sentence. Is the word* doesn't *or* couldn't*?*
- *Does the word* couldn't *take the place of the words* could not*?*
- *What letters are missing in* couldn't*?*

Part B: Follow the directions in Part B of the Beginning section.

Part C: Tell students they will write contractions that make pairs of words shorter. Read the words in the box. Then, read aloud the first sentence. Ask students to repeat the underlined words. Ask questions about the phrase to help students choose the correct contraction. Have them write and say the word. Read aloud the remaining sentences and pause to allow students time to write their answers.

Advanced

Part A: Distribute page 91. Direct students to look at the picture of the boy and girl. Slowly read the sentences aloud and have students repeat them. Invite students to talk about the picture. Tell students that *couldn't* is a contraction that is a short form for the words *could not*. Remind them that the apostrophe, the little mark in the word, shows that a letter or letters are missing.

Parts B and C: Read aloud the directions. Ask students to skim the page to see if they have a question about any of the words. Have students complete the page independently.

EXTENSION

Write the following contractions on the board: *I'll, let's, she'll,* and *it's.* Say sentences that use the pairs of words corresponding to these contractions. Challenge students to repeat the sentences using contractions.

Contractions

A. Read the sentences.

Kate **could not** catch Juan.

Kate **couldn't** catch Juan.

B. Draw lines to match words with the contraction.

1. is not   hasn't

2. has not   can't

3. cannot   isn't

C. Write a word from the box that can take the place of the underlined words.

doesn't	wasn't	didn't	wouldn't

4. Kate <u>was not</u> fast enough. _____

5. Juan <u>would not</u> stop. _____

6. Kate <u>did not</u> keep running. _____

7. She <u>does not</u> want to run again. _____

Prefixes

INTRODUCTION

Invite a volunteer who is wearing a tennis shoe to untie it and take it off. Write *untie* on the board. Now, ask the volunteer to put the shoe on and retie it. Now write *retie* on the board. Ask students how the words are alike and different. Help them realize that the first two letters are different. Explain that small word parts, called prefixes, can be added to the beginning of some words to change their meaning. Tell students that the word part *un* means "not," so *untie* means "not tie." Continue to explain that *re* means "again," so *retie* means "to tie again."

Beginning

Part A: Distribute page 93. Direct students to look at the picture of the boy. Read the sentences aloud and have students repeat them. Ask the following questions about the picture and sentences:
* *This boy is not happy. How can you tell this? Show me what his face looks like.*
* *What word in dark print means "not happy"? Point to it.*
* *Is the boy building the fence again?*
* *What word in dark print means "to build again"? Point to it.*

Tell students that *unhappy* means "not happy," and *rebuild* means "to build again." Remind them that the small word parts *re* and *un* are prefixes.

Part B: Tell students they will write words that match definitions. Read aloud the first definition. Then, have students point to the words in dark print in the sentences above. Ask questions that help students choose and write the word *rebuild*. Repeat with the second definition.

Part C: Tell students they will complete sentences by writing words that have prefixes. Slowly read the words in the box as students point to them and repeat them. Pantomime each word. Then, read the first sentence. Ask questions that help students use context clues to choose the correct word. Guide students to write *unwrap* on the line and mark it mark it off the word list. Continue the process with the remaining sentences.

Intermediate

Part A: Follow the directions in Part A of the Beginning section, but substitute these questions:
* *What word in dark print means "not happy"?*
* *What word in dark print means "to build again"?*

Part B: Follow the directions in Part B of the Beginning section.

Part C: Tell students they will write words that have prefixes to complete sentences. Slowly read the words in the box as students point to them and repeat them. Pantomime each word. Then, read aloud the first sentence. Ask questions that help students use context clues to choose the correct word. Guide students to write *unwrap* on the line and mark it off the word list. Read aloud the remaining sentences and pause to allow students time to write their answers.

Advanced

Part A: Distribute page 93. Direct students to look at the picture of the boy. Read the sentences aloud and have students repeat them. Invite students to talk about the picture. Tell students that *unhappy* means "not happy," and *rebuild* means "to build again." Remind them that the small word parts *re* and *un* are prefixes.

Parts B and C: Read aloud the directions. Ask students to skim the page to see if they have a question about any of the words. Have students complete the page independently.

EXTENSION

Write the following words on the board: *reopen, rewrite, rewind, uneven, unsafe,* and *unbutton.* Read aloud the words and help students understand them. Then, assign a word to partners. Have the pair pantomime the words for others to guess.

Prefixes

A. Read the sentences.

Tim was **unhappy**.

He had to **rebuild** the fence.

B. Write a word that matches each meaning. Use the words in dark print above.

1. to build again _____

2. not happy _____

C. Write a word from the box to complete each sentence.

retie	reread	reheat	unlock	unwrap

3. Jack will _____ the gift.

4. Ben wants to _____ the book.

5. Use the key to _____ the door.

6. I need to _____ my shoe.

7. Hau will _____ his cold pizza.

Suffixes

INTRODUCTION

Write *thankful* on the board. Explain the meaning and ask students what they are thankful for. Next, write *friendly* on the board and have students name ways they are friendly. Then, underline the suffixes in each word. Point out that small word parts, called suffixes, can be added to the end of some words to change their meaning. Tell students that the word part *ful* means "full of," so *thankful* means "full of thanks." Continue to explain that *ly* means "done in a certain way," so *friendly* means "done in a way that is like a friend."

Beginning

Part A: Distribute page 95. Direct students to look at the picture of the fish. Read the sentence aloud and have students repeat it. Ask the following questions about the picture and sentence:
• *Is this fish swimming in a slow way?*
• *What word in dark print means "in a slow way"? Point to it.*
• *Is the fish beautiful?*
• *What word in dark print means "full of beauty"? Point to it.*

Tell students that *beautiful* means "full of beauty," and *slowly* means "in a slow way." Remind them that the small word parts *ful* and *ly* are suffixes.

Part B: Tell students they will write words that match definitions. Read each definition and ask questions that help students find and write the corresponding word with a suffix from Part A.

Part C: Tell students they will complete sentences by writing words that have suffixes. Slowly read the words in the box as students point to them and repeat them. Pantomime each word. Then, read the first sentence. Ask questions that help students use context clues to choose the correct word. Guide students to write *quietly* on the line and mark it off the word list. Continue the process with the remaining sentences.

Intermediate

Part A: Follow the directions in Part A of the Beginning section, but substitute these questions:
• *What word in dark print means "full of beauty"?*
• *What word in dark print means "in a slow way"?*

Part B: Follow the directions in the Beginning section.

Part C: Tell students they will write words that have suffixes to complete sentences. Slowly read the words in the box as students point to them and repeat them. Pantomime each word. Then, read aloud the first sentence. Ask questions that help students use context clues to choose the correct word. Guide students to write *quietly* on the line and mark it off the word list. Read aloud the remaining sentences and pause to allow students time to write their answers.

Advanced

Part A: Distribute page 95. Direct students to look at the picture of the fish. Read the sentence aloud and have students repeat it. Invite students to talk about the picture. Tell students that *beautiful* means "full of beauty," and *slowly* means "in a slow way." Remind them that the small word parts *ful* and *ly* are suffixes.

Parts B and C: Read aloud the directions. Ask students to skim the page to see if they have a question about any of the words. Have students complete the page independently.

EXTENSION

Invite volunteers to demonstrate movements for the following words: *slowly, quickly, softly, happily,* and *loudly.*

Suffixes

A. Read the sentence.

The **beautiful** fish swam **slowly**.

B. Write a word that matches each meaning. Use the words in dark print above.

1. full of beauty _____

2. in a slow way _____

C. Write a word from the box to complete each sentence.

| helpful | playful | joyful | quickly | quietly |

3. The people talked _____ in the library.

4. The team was _____ when they won the game.

5. The dog ran _____ after the cat.

6. The _____ kitten chased the toy.

7. A _____ person told Rick when the bus would come.

Community

INTRODUCTION

Gather items that represent places in a community, such as a stamped letter to symbolize the post office and something with a price tag to symbolize a store. Hold each item up and lead students in a discussion of where each could be found. Write the names of the places on the board as they are identified. Challenge students to name other places not represented. Tell students that all of the places can be found in a community.

 Invite students to tell about a place they like to visit in a community in their native country.

Beginning

Part A: Distribute page 97. Direct students to look at the picture of the street scene. Read the sentence aloud and have students repeat it. Invite groups of students to name the places they know and share experiences of visiting those places. Ask the following questions about the picture:
• *Can you find a place to shop in this community? Point to it.*
• *Can you find a place where people live? Point to it.*
• *Can you find a place where people work? Point to it.*

Part B: Tell students that they will label places in a community. Have students put their finger on number *1* and listen as you read the word *park*. Have students point to the word and repeat it. Ask questions that help students find the symbol for a park on the map. Have students write the number *1* beside the park on the map. Continue the process with each place.

Intermediate

Part A: Follow the directions in Part A of the Beginning section, but substitute these questions:
• *Can you shop in a clothes store or a restaurant?*
• *Can you live in an apartment or a store?*
• *What place does the picture show?*

Part B: Tell students that they will label places in a community. Read aloud each word in the list. Have students point to the word and repeat it. Ask questions that help students find the symbol for a park on the map. Have students write the number *1* beside the park on the map. Identify places on the map and lead discussions about each picture to be sure students understand each community place. Then, have students work with a partner to complete the page.

Advanced

Part A: Distribute page 97. Direct students to look at the picture of the street scene. Read the sentence aloud and have students repeat it. Invite students to talk about the picture. Challenge students to name stores they know like the ones shown in the picture. Remind students that these places can be found in most communities.

Part B: Read aloud the directions. Ask students to skim the page to see if they have a question about any of the words or pictures. Have students complete the page independently.

EXTENSION

Invite students to draw a picture of a place in their town they like to visit. Help them write a sentence describing it.

Community

A. Read the sentence.

A **community** has places to shop, work, and play.

B. Write the number on the map to label the place.

1. park	4. school	7. post office	10. restaurant
2. barber	5. hospital	8. shoe store	11. clothes store
3. library	6. fire station	9. supermarket	12. fruit market

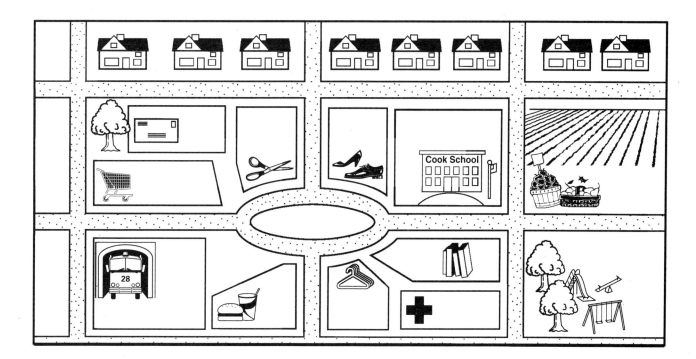

Days of the Week

INTRODUCTION

Display a classroom calendar and point out the days of the week. Teach students this revised version of the song "Frère Jacques":

Sunday, Monday, Tuesday, Wednesday,
Are some days of the week.
Followed by Thursday, Friday, and Saturday.
Seven days make a week!

 Invite students to say the names of the days of the week in their native language.

Beginning

Part A: Distribute page 99. Direct students to look at the calendar that shows the days of the week. Read the sentence aloud and have students repeat it. Ask the following questions:
• *What is the first day of the week? Point to it.*
• *Is this day Sunday?*
• *Are there six days in a week?*
• *Are there seven days in a week?*

Review the days of the week in order and have students repeat them. Remind students there are seven days in a week.

Part B: Tell students that they will answer questions about the days of the week. Point out that the calendar will help them remember the order. Review the names of the days of the week as students point to them and repeat them. Then, read aloud each question. Guide students to find the answer using the calendar and to write the day on the line.

Intermediate

Part A: Follow the directions in Part A of the Beginning section, but substitute these questions:
• *Is the first day of the week Sunday or Thursday?*
• *Is the last day of the week Friday or Saturday?*
• *How many days of the week are there?*

Part B: Tell students that they will answer questions about the days of the week. Point out that the calendar will help them remember the order. Review the days of the week. Then, read aloud each question. Pause between the questions so that students can write their answers.

Advanced

Part A: Distribute page 99. Direct students to look at the calendar that shows the days of the week. Read the sentence aloud and have students repeat it. Invite students to talk about the calendar. Review the days of the week in order and have students repeat them. Remind students there are seven days in a week.

Part B: Read aloud the directions. Ask students to skim the page to see if they have a question about any of the words. Have students complete the page independently.

EXTENSION

Together, create a weekly calendar that shows the activities the class attends, such as a library visit or computer lab.

Name _____ Date _____

Days of the Week

A. Read the sentence.

Sunday	Monday	Tuesday	Wednesday	Thursday	Friday	Saturday

There are seven **days** in a week.

B. Use the calendar above to answer the questions.

1. What day comes after Tuesday? _____

2. What day comes before Friday? _____

3. What day comes after Sunday? _____

4. What day comes before Wednesday? _____

5. What two days start with the letter **S**? _____

_____

6. What days do you come to school? _____

_____

_____

7. What two days do you stay home from school?

_____

_____

Family Words

INTRODUCTION

Display a picture of your family. Explain who the people are using the words *father, mother, sister, brother,* and so on. Write each word on the board. Then lead students in a discussion of a family. Point out that a family can be made of two people, like a grandmother and a granddaughter, as well as made of lots of people that include aunts, uncles, and cousins.

 Invite students to share the words for family members in their native language as you point to the ones listed on the board.

Beginning

Part A: Distribute page 101. Direct students to look at the picture of the family. Explain what is happening in the picture. Read the sentence aloud and have students repeat it. Ask the following questions about the picture:

- *Do you see someone who might be a father? Point to him.*
- *Do you see someone who might be a mother? Point to her.*
- *Do you see someone who might be a brother? Point to him.*
- *Do you see someone who might be a sister? Point to her.*

Review the list of family words on the board.

Part B: Tell students that the family words are all mixed up. Explain that they need to write the words correctly and then write the name of someone who is related in that way to them. Have students point to each word in the box as you read it aloud. Have students repeat the words. Then, invite a volunteer to call out the letters of a word as you write them on the board. Model how to search the list for the word. Write the word correctly and say the word for students to repeat. Allow them time to write a family member's name. Continue the process with each word.

Intermediate

Part A: Follow the directions in Part A of the Beginning section.

Part B: Tell students that the family words are all mixed up. Explain that they need to write the words correctly and then write the name of someone who is related in that way to them. Have students point to each word in the box as you read it aloud. Have students repeat the words. Invite a volunteer to call out the letters of a word as you write them on the board. Model how to search the list for the word. Write the word correctly and say the word for students to repeat. Allow them time to write a family member's name. Have students work with a partner to complete the page.

Advanced

Part A: Distribute page 101. Direct students to look at the picture of the family. Read the sentence aloud and have students repeat it. Invite students to talk about the picture. Have them speculate who the family members could be. Review the list of family words on the board.

Part B: Read aloud the directions. Ask students to skim the page to see if they have a question about any of the words. Have students complete the page independently.

EXTENSION

Invite students to draw a picture of a time their family had fun. Help students label the picture with family words. Encourage students to share the picture with the class.

Family Words

A. Read the sentence.

A **family** has fun together.

B. The letters are mixed up. Write the words for people in a family. Then, write the name of someone in your family who is this kind of person.

mother	father	aunt	grandmother
sister	brother	uncle	grandfather

1. r a h t e f _____

2. r t i s e s _____

3. u t a n _____

4. r n m t e g a d o h r _____

5. d a g n r f t e h a r _____

6. h o m r e t _____

7. t e r r h o b _____

8. c l u n e _____

Furniture

INTRODUCTION

Make labels for the names of the furniture in the classroom. Hold each one up, say the name, and have students repeat it. Mime using the furniture. Challenge a volunteer to tape the label to the furniture and repeat the name. Next, invite students to name other furniture. Write the names on the board and have students draw a picture of the furniture.

 Ask students to draw a picture of a piece of furniture they might find in their native country, but that people in the United States would not know. Have them display the picture, name it, and tell its use.

Beginning

Part A: Distribute page 103. Direct students to look at the picture of the people and the truck. Read the sentence aloud and have students repeat it. Explain that the people are movers, and they are carrying a sofa. Then, invite a pair of students to pantomime carrying a heavy sofa. Ask the following questions about the picture:
• *Are the men carrying furniture?*
• *Are the men carrying a sofa? Point to it.*

Part B: Tell students they will write words that name furniture. Identify the picture of the crib. Have students repeat the word. Tell students that *crib* is spelled *c, r, i, b*. Help them find the word in the list, write it on the line, and cross out the word once it is chosen. Continue the process with the remaining pictures by identifying the names of the furniture and their spellings.

Intermediate

Part A: Follow the directions in Part A of the Beginning section, but substitute these questions:
• *Are the men carrying furniture or food?*
• *Are they carrying a sofa or a sun?*

Part B: Tell students they will write words that name furniture. Then, have them point to each word in the box as you read it aloud. Ask students to repeat the word after you. Identify the picture of the crib. Have students repeat the word. Tell students that *crib* is spelled *c, r, i, b*. Help them find the word and write *crib* on the line. Help students identify the names of the remaining furniture. Ask students to work with a partner to complete the page.

Advanced

Part A: Distribute page 103. Direct students to look at the picture of the people and the truck. Read the sentence aloud and have students repeat it. Invite students to talk about the men and their actions. Then, invite a pair of students to pantomime carrying a heavy sofa.

Part B: Read aloud the directions. Ask students to skim the page to see if they have a question about any of the words or pictures. Have students complete the page independently.

EXTENSION

Review the list of furniture names on the board. Brainstorm other items students may now know. Have partners categorize the furniture according to the room they would find it in a house.

Furniture

A. Read the sentence.

The men move the **furniture**.

B. Write the name that matches the picture.

crib	sofa	table	chair	shelves
bed	desk	dresser	lamp	

1.

_____

2.

_____

3.

_____

4.

_____

5.

_____

6.

_____

7.

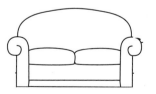

_____

8.

_____

9.

_____

Land and Water

INTRODUCTION

Think of a local landform or body of water that students would be familiar with. If possible, display a picture of it or find information about it on the Internet. Lead students in a discussion of characteristics of the place and activities they can enjoy there. Write the name of the landform or body of water on the board and have students repeat it. Invite them to name other places they know about. Draw pictures, write the names on the board, and discuss the characteristics of each.

 Invite students to say the names of the landforms and bodies of water in their native language.

 The homonyms *plain* and *plane* may confuse students. Write *plain* and *plane* on the board and explain their meanings. Then, say simple sentences that provide context clues of the word's use. *(The plain has good soil. We fly in a plane.)* Invite students to clap when they hear a sentence in which *plain* refers to a kind of land. Also explain that the word *plain* has two different meanings. Then, say simple sentences that provide context clues of the word's use. *(The plain is flat and covered with grass. This shirt is very plain.)* Invite students to clap when they hear a sentence in which *plain* refers to a kind of land.

Beginning

Part A: Distribute page 105. Direct students to look at the picture of the land and water. Read the sentence aloud and have students repeat it. Have students point to each label as you read it aloud. Have them repeat the word. Lead students in a discussion of characteristics of each place. Add the landform or body of water to the list on the board. Next, ask the following questions about the picture:
- *Where is the mountain? peninsula? plateau? valley? plain? island? Point to it.*
- *Where is the lake? river? ocean? Point to it.*

Part B: Tell students they will write words that name kinds of land or water. Identify the picture of the island. Have students repeat the word. Tell students that *island* is spelled *i, s, l, a, n, d.* Help them find the word in the list, write it on the line, and cross out the word once it is chosen. Continue the process with the remaining pictures by identifying the names of the landforms and bodies of water and their spellings.

Intermediate

Part A: Follow the directions in Part A of the Beginning section.

Part B: Tell students they will write words that name kinds of land or water. Then, have them point to each word in the box as you read it aloud. Ask students to repeat the word after you. Identify the picture of the island. Have students repeat the word. Tell students that *island* is spelled *i, s, l, a, n, d.* Help them find the word and write *island* on the line. Help students identify the names of the remaining landforms and bodies of water. Ask students to work with a partner to complete the page.

Advanced

Part A: Distribute page 105. Direct students to look at the picture of the land and water. Read the sentence aloud and have students repeat it. Invite students to talk about the picture. Challenge students to name the characteristics of each kind of land or water. Add the landform or body of water to the list on the board.

Part B: Read aloud the directions. Ask students to skim the page to see if they have a question about any of the words or pictures. Have students complete the page independently.

EXTENSION

Invite students to draw a picture of their native country. Encourage them to include landforms and bodies of water. Help them label the areas on their map.

Land and Water

A. Read the sentence.

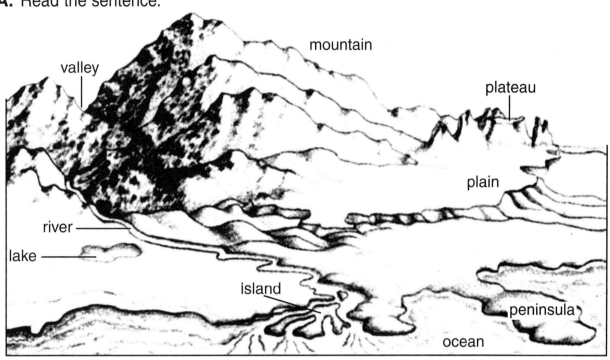

Many kinds of **land** and **water** shape the Earth.

B. Write the name that matches the picture.

plain	ocean	river	mountain	island	lake

1.

_____

2.

_____

3.

_____

4.

_____

5.

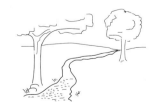

_____

6.

_____

Machines

INTRODUCTION

Arrange to take students on a tour of the kitchen in the cafeteria. Say each appliance name and have students repeat it. Demonstrate how the different appliances work and discuss their uses.

 Invite students to say the names of different machines in their native language.

 Explain that many people refer to the telephone as a *phone*. Next, tell students that "get the phone" is an idiom they may find confusing. It means "to answer the phone," not "to carry the phone to a different place."

Beginning

Part A: Distribute page 107. Direct students to look at the pictures of the kitchen and the living room. Read the sentence aloud and have students repeat it. Lead students in a discussion of the names of the rooms and machines they see. Have them identify which machines are used for work and which are used for play. Ask the following questions about the pictures:
• *Which room is the living room? Point to it.*
• *Where is the computer? radio? telephone? television? Point to it.*
• *Which room is the kitchen? Point to it.*
• *Where is the stove? refrigerator? microwave? Point to it.*

Part B: Tell students that they will use the words used as labels from Part A to complete sentences. Read aloud the first sentence. Ask questions that help students use context clues to identify the missing word. Guide students to find the word in Part A and write it on the line. Continue the process with each sentence.

Intermediate

Part A: Follow the directions in Part A of the Beginning section.

Part B: Tell students that they will use the words used as labels from Part A to complete sentences. Read aloud the first sentence. Ask questions that help students use context clues to identify the missing word. Pause between each sentence so that students can write their answers.

Advanced

Part A: Distribute page 107. Direct students to look at the pictures of the kitchen and the living room. Read the sentence aloud and have students repeat it. Invite students to talk about the pictures. Have them identify which machines are used for work and which are used for play.

Part B: Read aloud the directions. Ask students to skim the page to see if they have a question about any of the words. Have students complete the page independently.

EXTENSION

Divide students into groups and assign each a room in a house. Have them brainstorm and draw a list of machines they might find in that room. As students share their drawings, have them identify which machines would be used for work and which would be used for play.

Machines

A. Read the sentence.

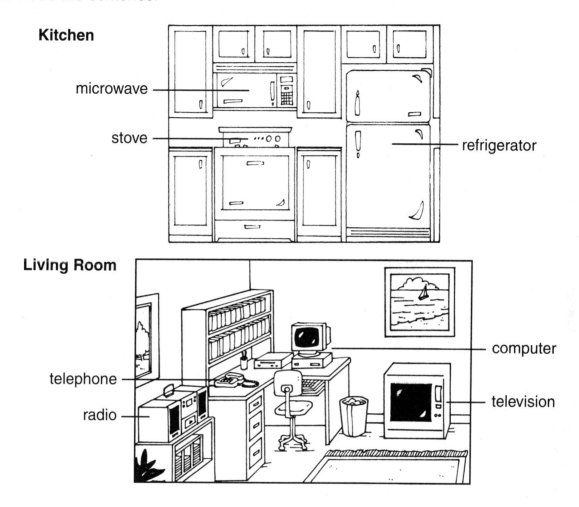

Kitchen

microwave

stove

refrigerator

Living Room

telephone

radio

computer

television

Machines make work easy and play fun.

B. Write a word from above to complete each sentence.

1. We watch movies on a _____.

2. We listen to music on a _____.

3. We type words on a _____.

4. We talk on a _____.

5. We keep food cold in a _____.

6. We cook food on a _____ and in a _____.

Money

INTRODUCTION
Provide a handful of coins and invite students to sort them. Afterwards, name the coins, tell their value, and have students look at both sides of the coins. Tell students that the coins are some examples of American money. Encourage students to tell about experiences they have had buying things.

 Invite students to bring to class several coins from their native country.

Beginning
Part A: Distribute page 109. Direct students to look at the pictures of the coins. Read the sentence aloud and have students repeat it. Review the coins, their values, and word names. Explain that there are several kinds of American money, but the ones they will learn now are coins. Ask the following questions about the sentence and pictures:
• *Which coin is the penny? nickel? dime? quarter? Point to it.*
• *Which word in the sentence is* money*? Point to it.*

Part B: Tell students that they will count groups of coins to find their amounts. Identify each coin in the first group and tell its value as students point to it and repeat the name. Then, model how to count the coins by adding on. Repeat the pattern and have students write the amounts. Continue the process with each group of coins.

Intermediate
Part A: Follow the directions in Part A of the Beginning section.

Part B: Tell students that they will count groups of coins to find their amounts. Invite a volunteer to name the coins and their values in the first group. Then, model how to count the coins by adding on. Pause at the last coin for students to say the final value. Repeat with the remaining groups of coins.

Advanced
Part A: Distribute page 109. Direct students to look at the pictures of the coins. Read the sentence aloud and have students repeat it. Review the coins, their values, and word names. Explain that there are several kinds of American money, but the ones they will learn now are coins.

Part B: Read aloud the directions. Ask students to skim the page to see if they have a question about any of the pictures. Have students complete the page independently.

EXTENSION
Write price tags for small items, such as pencils and pens. Have students count out the coins needed to purchase the items.

Name _____   Date _____

Money

A. Read the sentence.

   1 cent   5 cents   10 cents   25 cents
    1¢   5¢   10¢   25¢

Money can buy things.

B. Count on to find the total amount.

1.

_____¢ _____¢ _____¢ _____¢ _____¢

2.

_____¢ _____¢ _____¢ _____¢

3.

_____¢ _____¢ _____¢ _____¢

4.

_____¢ _____¢ _____¢ _____¢ _____¢

School Rooms

INTRODUCTION

Take students on a tour of the school. As you point out the rooms, say the names and have students repeat them. Lead students in a discussion of the kinds of equipment they find in the room. Make note of rooms that have the same equipment and discuss how the equipment might be used in each room.

 Invite students to share how the schools in their native country are the same as and different from those in the United States.

Beginning

Part A: Distribute page 111. Direct students to look at the map of the school. Read the sentence aloud and have students repeat it. Review each room name and the equipment found in each. Remind students of the ones they visited. Ask the following questions about the sentence and map:
- *Which room is the art room? cafeteria? music room? gym? office? nurse? computer room? Point to it.*
- *How many classrooms do you count?*
- *Which word in the sentence is* school? *rooms? Point to it.*

Part B: Tell students that they will look at the pictures of items found in a school and write those numbers on the map to show in which room the items would be found. Explain that a number can be used in more than one room. Then, have students put their finger on the picture of the computer. Say the name and have students repeat it. Ask questions that help students identify the rooms in which a computer might be found. Have them write a *1* in those rooms. Continue the process with the remaining pictures.

Intermediate

Part A: Follow the directions in Part A of the Beginning section.

Part B: Tell students that they will look at the pictures of items found in a school and write those numbers on the map to show in which room the items would be found. Explain that a number can be used in more than one room. Then, have students put their finger on the picture of the computer. Say the name and have students repeat it. Ask questions that help students identify the rooms in which a computer might be found. Have them write a *1* in those rooms. Next, identify the remaining pictures and have students repeat the names. Ask students to work with a partner to complete the page.

Advanced

Part A: Distribute page 111. Direct students to look at the map of the school. Read the sentence aloud and have students repeat it. Review each room and the equipment found in each.

Part B: Read aloud the directions. Ask students to skim the page to see if they have a question about any of the words or pictures. Have students complete the page independently.

EXTENSION

Have partners make a map of their school. Encourage them to label the rooms and draw a picture of one kind of equipment they found in each.

School Rooms

A. Read the sentence.

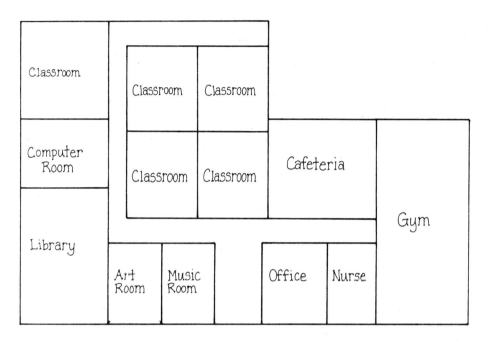

A **school** has different **rooms**.

B. Where does each item belong? Write the number on the map above. You may use some numbers more than once.

Senses

INTRODUCTION

Pass out a cracker to each student. Ask the following questions:
- *What does the cracker look like?*
- *What does the cracker smell like?*
- *What does the cracker feel like?*
- *Take a bite of the cracker. What does it sound like?*
- *What does the cracker taste like?*

As students finish the crackers, discuss that the students used their senses to learn about the cracker. Have students point to the body parts they used. Write these names on the board as they are identified. Then, point out the sense associated with each body part.

 Invite students to name the body parts and senses in their native language.

 The homograph *sense* may confuse students. First, explain that *sense* has two meanings. Say simple sentences that provide context clues of the word's use. *(You have a good sense of smell. That does not make sense.)* Have students clap their hands if they hear a sentence in which the word is used in reference to the body. Next, write *sense* and *cents* on the board and explain their meanings. Then, say simple sentences that provide context clues of the word's use. *(I use my eyes for my sense of seeing. Lena has fifty cents.)* Invite students to clap when they hear a sentence in which the word *sense* refers to the body.

Beginning

Part A: Distribute page 113. Direct students to look at the body parts. Read the sentence aloud and have students repeat it. Explain that the different body parts help them learn about the world. Read aloud the sense names as students point to the pictures. Ask the following questions about the pictures:
- *What do you smell with? Point to it.*
- *What do you hear with? Point to it.*
- *What do you see with? Point to it.*
- *What do you touch with? Point to it.*
- *What do you taste with? Point to it.*

Remind students that there are five senses. Say a sense and have students point to the body part that is associated with it.

Part B: Tell students that they will write the sense name that will help them learn about pictured items. Have students point to the picture of the food as you name it. Ask questions that help students determine they would use their sense of taste to learn about food. Direct them to find the word *tasting* in Part A and to write it under the picture of the food. Continue the process with the remaining pictures.

Intermediate

Part A: Follow the directions in Part A of the Beginning section, but substitute these questions:
- *Would you use your nose or your eyes to smell with?*
- *Would you use your tongue or your eyes to taste with?*
- *Would you use your ears or your nose to hear with?*
- *Would you use your hand or your ear to touch with?*
- *Would you use your ears or your eyes to see with?*

Part B: Tell students that they will write the sense name that will help them learn about pictured items. Have students point to the picture of the food as you name it. Ask questions that help students determine they would use their sense of taste to learn about food. Direct them to find the word *tasting* in Part A and to write it under the picture of the food. Then, help students identify the remaining pictures. Have students work with a partner to complete the page.

Advanced

Part A: Distribute page 113. Direct students to look at the body parts. Read the sentence aloud and have students repeat it. Explain that the different body parts help them learn about the world. Read aloud the sense names as student point to the pictures. Remind students there are five senses.

Part B: Read aloud the directions. Ask students to skim the page to see if they have a question about any of the pictures. Have students complete the page independently.

EXTENSION

Group students and assign each a sense. Have them draw items or situations in which they would use that sense to learn about something. Invite each group to show their items and challenge the other students to identify the sense.

Name _____   Date _____

Senses

A. Read the sentence.

touching   seeing   smelling   tasting   hearing

There are five **senses**.

B. Look at each picture. Which sense would you use the most? Write the sense under the picture.

1.

_____

2.

_____

3.

_____

4.

_____

5.

_____

6.

_____

7.

_____

8.

_____

9.

_____

Shapes

INTRODUCTION

Distribute shape blocks and challenge students to make a shape pattern. Help students name the shapes in their patterns.

 Invite students to identify the pattern using their native language.

Beginning

Part A: Distribute page 115. Direct students to look at the picture frames. Read the sentence aloud and have students repeat it. Say each shape name as students point to that frame and repeat the name. Ask the following questions about the sentence and pictures:

- *Which frame looks like a square? rectangle? circle? triangle? Point to it.*
- *Which word in the sentence is* shapes? *Point to it.*

Remind students that a square, rectangle, circle, and triangle are all shapes.

Part B: Tell students that they will count shapes and write the number in a chart. Point out the chart and how to use it. Have students point to the circle in the chart. Model how to find and count circles in the bird and record the answer. Then, have students point to the square. Ask questions that help them count the squares in the bird and record the answer. Continue the process with the remaining shapes.

Intermediate

Part A: Follow the directions in Part A of the Beginning section.

Part B: Tell students that they will count shapes and write the number in a chart. Point out the chart and how to use it. Have students point to the circle in the table. Model how to find and count circles in the bird and record the answer. Identify the remaining shapes. Have students work with a partner to complete the chart.

Advanced

Part A: Distribute page 115. Direct students to look at the picture frames. Read the sentence aloud and have students repeat it. Invite students to discuss the picture and name the shapes they see.

Part B: Read aloud the directions. Ask students to skim the page to see if they have a question about any of the words or pictures. Model how to count the circles and record the answer in the chart. Then, have students complete the page independently.

EXTENSION

Invite students to make pictures using shape blocks. Have partners work together to create a chart showing the total number of each shape.

Shapes

A. Read the sentence.

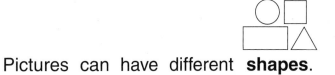

Pictures can have different **shapes**.

B. How many of each shape do you see? Complete the table.

Shape Bird

Shape	⬤ circle	☐ square	▭ rectangle	△ triangle
Number				

Sports

INTRODUCTION

Take students outside or to the gym to play a game they enjoy. On the return to the classroom, have students name the sport and the equipment they used. Tell students they were playing a sport and discuss the meaning of the word *sport*. Have students name sports in which they participate.

 Invite students to name and describe a sport enjoyed in their native country.

Beginning

Part A: Distribute page 117. Direct students to look at the picture. Read the sentence aloud and have students repeat it. Ask the following questions about the sentence and picture:
• *Are the students running?*
• *Are the students chasing a soccer ball?*
• *What word in the sentence is* sport*? Point to it.*

Lead students in a discussion of why it is healthy to participate in a sport.

Part B: Tell students they will write words that name sports. Identify the picture of the girl biking. Have students repeat the word. Tell students that *biking* is spelled *b, i, k, i, n, g*. Help them find the word in the list, write it on the line, and cross out the word once it is chosen. Continue the process with the remaining pictures by identifying the names of the sports and their spellings.

Intermediate

Part A: Follow the directions in Part A of the Beginning section, but substitute these questions:
• *Are the students running?*
• *Are they playing with a ball or a bat?*
• *What is the word in bold print?*

Part B: Tell students they will write words that name sports. Then, have them point to each word in the box as you read it aloud. Ask students to repeat the word after you. Identify the picture of the girl biking. Have students repeat the word. Tell students that *biking* is spelled *b, i, k, i, n, g*. Have them find the word in the list, write it on the line, and cross out the word once it is chosen. Help students identify the names of the remaining sports in the box. Ask students to work with a partner to complete the page.

Advanced

Part A: Distribute page 117. Direct students to look at the picture. Read the sentence aloud and have students repeat it. Invite students to discuss the picture and name the equipment the students are using. Lead students in a discussion of why it is good to participate in sports.

Part B: Read aloud the directions. Ask students to skim the page to see if they have a question about any of the words or pictures. Have students complete the page independently.

EXTENSION

Ask students to draw a picture of themselves participating in a favorite sport. Encourage them to include all the equipment they will use. As students share the drawings, help them name the sport and the equipment.

Time

A. Read the sentences.

The clock shows 4:00.

It is **time** to feed the dog.

B. Write the time.

1.

_____

2.

_____

3.

_____

4.

_____

5.

_____

6.

_____

---

7. Write the times in order.

_____ _____ _____ _____ _____ _____

Weather

INTRODUCTION

Invite students to draw a picture to show the day's weather. As students share their pictures, help them identify the words associated with the weather and write them on the board. Point to the words as you say them and have students repeat them.

 Invite students to tell what kind of weather was common in their native country.

 Students may find the idiom "I'm feeling under the weather!" confusing. Explain that the phrase means that the person is feeling sick.

Beginning

Part A: Distribute page 121. Direct students to look at the picture of the students. Read the sentences aloud and have students repeat them. Ask the following questions about the sentences and picture:

- *Is it sunny in the picture?*
- *Is it raining in the picture?*
- *What kinds of things do people need if it rains? Point to them.*
- *Which word in the sentence is* weather*? Point to it.*

Invite students to name other kinds of weather. Write the words on the board and have students repeat them.

Part B: Tell students that they will write words that name kinds of weather. Have students point to the picture of the clouds. Say *clouds* and have students repeat it. Tell students that *clouds* is spelled *c, l, o, u, d, s.* Help them find the word in the list, write it on the line, and cross out the word once it is chosen. Continue the process with the remaining pictures by identifying the kinds of weather and their spellings.

Intermediate

Part A: Follow the directions in Part A of the Beginning section, but substitute these questions:
- *Is it sunny or rainy in the picture?*
- *Do people wear jackets or raincoats when it rains?*
- *What does the word in bold print say?*

Part B: Tell students that they will write words that name kinds of weather. Have students point to the picture of the clouds. Say *clouds* and have students repeat it. Tell students that *clouds* is spelled *c, l, o, u, d, s.* Have them find the word in the list, write it on the line, and cross out the word once it is chosen. Then, help students identify the names of the remaining weather types in the box. Ask students to work with a partner to complete the page.

Advanced

Part A: Distribute page 121. Direct students to look at the picture of the students. Read the sentences aloud and have students repeat them. Invite students to discuss the picture. Then, challenge students to name other kinds of weather. Write the words on the board and have students repeat them.

Part B: Read aloud the directions. Ask students to skim the page to see if they have a question about any of the pictures or words. Have students complete the page independently.

EXTENSION

Track the weather for one week. Discuss the changes the students noticed and how the weather affected their choice of clothing.

Name _____   Date _____

Weather

A. Read the sentences.

What is the **weather** like today?

It will rain.

B. Write the name that matches the picture.

| sun | rain | snow | wind | clouds | lightning |

1.

_____

2.

_____

3.

_____

4.

_____

5.

_____

6.

_____

Dear _____,

You are doing a great job!
Keep up the good work.

_____   _____

Great job, _____!

You know your

_____.

The United States has other symbols, too.
The eagle is an important symbol.
The eagle is a large bird.
It is very strong, too.
Americans like to think they are strong like the eagle.

You can find the American flag at school.
You can also find one at the post office.
Many people fly a flag on July Fourth, too.
July Fourth is a special American holiday.
It is the day Americans said they would not follow English rule.
The flag shows that people are proud.

The Liberty Bell is another symbol of the
United States.
It was made over two hundred years ago.
The bell has a big crack in it.
Long ago, Americans rang the bell when
they wanted to tell important news.
Some news was good.
Some news was bad.

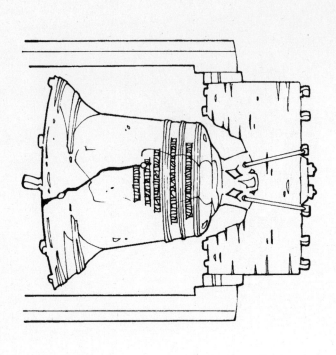

A symbol is something that has a special
meaning.
The United States has some symbols.
The American flag is one very special
symbol.
The American flag is red, white, and blue.
It has fifty white stars.
The stripes are red and white.

The Statue of Liberty is a symbol of freedom.
Long ago, many people left their countries.
They sailed across the ocean.
They came to live in the United States.
They wanted to be free and to have a
better life.
The Statue of Liberty was the first thing
they saw.
The statue became a special symbol for
them, too.

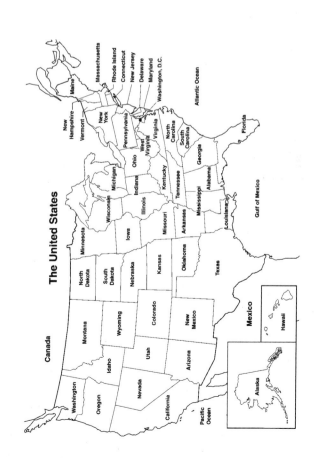

The United States is divided into states.
Some states have lots of mountains.
Some have hot deserts.
Other states are near the ocean.
Some states have a little of everything.
Can you find the state you live in?

The United States

Today, many people still come to the United States.
Just like long ago, they want to be free.
They want to have a better life.
It is hard work to learn the language.
It is hard to learn a new way of life.
But soon, these people will become Americans, too.
They will be proud of all American symbols.

Pinewood School

American Symbols

The world is a big place.
It has large areas of land and water.
There are many countries, too.
The United States is one of those countries.
The United States also has another name.
It is called America.

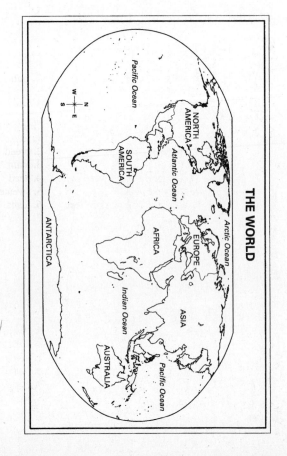

THE WORLD

ESL Grades 4–6

Answer Key

Page 5
1. on
2. in
3. beside
4. under

Page 6
1. middle
2. bottom
3. top
4. bottom
5. top
6. middle

Page 7
The directions are left, right, left.

Page 8
1. same
2. different
3. different
4. same
5. different
6. same

Page 9
Have students tell which animal they visited using the words *first*, *next*, and *last*.

Page 10
Check students' numbers. Have them say the number names.

Page 11
Check that students write the correct number name to match the numeral on the book spine.

Page 12
Check that students draw a line to the numerals in order from 1 to 20 through the maze.

Page 13
1. 70; seventy
2. 40; forty
3. 50; fifty
4. 90; ninety

Page 14
1. 200; two hundred
2. 500; five hundred
3. 700; seven hundred
4. 2,000; two thousand
5. 4,000; four thousand
6. 6,000; six thousand

Page 15
Check that students follow the letters alphabetically to complete the skateboard ramp. Also check to see that they write the capital letters in cursive.

Page 16
Check that students follow the letters alphabetically to complete the sailboat. Also check to see that they write the lowercase letters in cursive.

Page 17
Students color: Bb, Cc, Dd, Ff, Gg, Hh, Ii, Jj, Ll, Nn, Pp, Qq, Rr, Ss, Uu, Vv, Ww, Yy, Zz
The frog eats 19 flies.

Page 18
1. m
2. c
3. s
4. n
5. w
6. b
7. h
8. g
9. p

Page 19
1. t
2. b
3. s
4. p
5. j
6. c
7. h
8. s
9. w

Page 20
Check students' work.

Page 21
Check students' work.

Page 22
Check students' work.

Page 23
Check students' work.

Page 24
1. listen
2. say
3. raise hand
4. look

Page 25
Check that students circle the ball, underline the paint cans, write their name on the building, and color the apple.

Page 27
1. bat
2. cap
3. pan
4. map
5. gas

Page 29
1. nest
2. hen
3. desk
4. egg
5. vet

Page 31
1. pig
2. dig
3. pin
4. hit
5. clip
6. wig

Page 33
1. hot
2. pot
3. fox
4. top
5. dog
6. hop

Page 35
1. run
2. duck
3. up
4. bug
5. rug

Page 37
1. rake
2. gate
3. The students play a game.
4. The students made a cake.
5. The students are at the lake.

Page 39
1. quail
2. hay
3. rain
4. train
5. tray

Page 41
1. bee
2. leaf
3. The bee sits on a weed.
4. The sheep eat.
5. We wear shoes on our feet.

Page 43
1. five
2. pies
3. bike
4. kite
5. tie

Page 45
1. nose
2. rose
3. home
4. robe
5. globe

Page 47
1. road
2. doe
3. The doe saw a toad.
4. The man has a hoe.
5. The girl hurt her toe.

Page 49
1. flute
2. tune
3. tube
4. glue
5. mule

Page 51
1. fly
2. puppy
3. The puppy is in the city.
4. The baby did cry.
5. The sun is in the sky.

Page 53
1. barn
2. car
3. The car has a star.
4. I hear a harp.
5. Grandma has yarn.

Page 55
1. horse
2. corn
3. b
4. c
5. a

Page 57
1. fern
2. nurse
3. bird
4. purse
5. person
6. shirt

Page 59
1. tea
2. bread
3. team
4. head
5. sweater
6. jeans
7. thread
8. peach
Circle head, sweater, thread.

Page 61
1. hall
2. yawns
3. walks
4. saucer, au
5. paw, aw
6. ball, all
7. talk, al
8. faucet, au
9. chalk, al

Page 63
1. town
2. snow
3. cow
4. clown
5. crown
6. bowl
7. blow
8. mow
Circle bowl, blow, mow.

Page 65
1. city
2. cab
3. Answer order may vary: cent, fence, pencil, mice.
4. Answer order may vary: cut, can, corn, cat.

Page 67
1. garden
2. gerbil
3. Answer order may vary: gem, giant, cage, stage.
4. Answer order may vary: gum, gas, dog, wig.

Page 69
1. sugar
2. soap
3. cheese
4. s
5. z
6. sh
7. s
8. z
9. sh
10. s
11. z

Page 71
1. children
2. whisper
3. whistle
4. chair
5. chick

Page 73
1. shirt
2. that
3. thirteen
4. Look at those ships.
5. A shell is on the sand.
6. The rose has a thorn.

Page 75
1. boy
2. farm
3. goat
For **4–6**, answer order may vary.
4. Person: girl, vet
5. Place: kitchen, zoo, park
6. Thing: peach, truck, book

Page 77
1. Marco
2. South Street
3. Circle: marco; Marco
4. Circle: dr. smith; Dr. Smith
5. Circle: marco, cook road; Marco, Cook Road
6. Circle: oak library; Oak Library
7. Circle: mrs. kim; Mrs. Kim

Page 79
1. log
2. frogs
3. ducks
4. wings
5. flies
6. frog
7. lake

Page 81
1. runs
2. run
3. walk
4. eat
5. sees
6. sleeps
7. laugh

Page 83
1. climbed
2. pulled
3. visited
4. played
5. walked
6. talked
7. worked

Page 85
1. she
2. they
3. She
4. It
5. He
6. They

Page 87
1. biggest
2. big
3. bigger
4. slowest
5. bigger
6. tallest
7. soft

Page 89
1. foot
2. ball
3. rainbow
4. sailboat
5. lunchroom
6. birthday

Page 91
1. isn't
2. hasn't
3. can't
4. wasn't
5. wouldn't
6. didn't
7. doesn't

Page 93
1. rebuild
2. unhappy
3. unwrap
4. reread
5. unlock
6. retie
7. reheat

Page 95
1. beautiful
2. slowly
3. quietly
4. joyful
5. quickly
6. playful
7. helpful

Page 97
Check students' maps.

Page 99
1. Wednesday
2. Thursday
3. Monday
4. Tuesday
5. Sunday, Saturday
6. Monday, Tuesday, Wednesday, Thursday, Friday
7. Saturday, Sunday

Page 101
1. father
2. sister
3. aunt
4. grandmother
5. grandfather
6. mother
7. brother
8. uncle

Page 103
1. crib
2. chair
3. lamp
4. shelves
5. dresser
6. desk
7. sofa
8. table
9. bed

Page 105
1. island
2. lake
3. ocean
4. mountain
5. river
6. plain

Page 107
1. television
2. radio
3. computer
4. telephone
5. refrigerator
6. stove; microwave

Page 109
1. 5¢
2. 16¢
3. 35¢
4. 75¢

Page 111
Answers may vary.
1. classroom, computer room, library, office, nurse, cafeteria
2. art room, classroom
3. cafeteria
4. classroom, office, library
5. office, nurse
6. music room
7. nurse
8. library, classroom
9. gym

Page 113
1. tasting
2. seeing
3. hearing
4. smelling
5. touching
6. touching
7. seeing
8. hearing
9. smelling

Page 115
Circle: 2
Square: 5
Rectangle: 5
Triangle: 8

Page 117
1. biking
2. skiing
3. skateboarding
4. dancing
5. volleyball
6. football
7. baseball
8. tennis
9. basketball

Page 119
1. 9:45
2. 8:15
3. 8:00
4. 8:45
5. 9:30
6. 10:00
7. 8:00, 8:15, 8:45, 9:30, 9:45, 10:00

Page 121
1. clouds
2. rain
3. wind
4. lightning
5. snow
6. sun